GEORGIA WILDLIFE VIEWING GUIDE

BY JERRY MCCOLLUM,
BETSIE ROTHERMEL, & CHUCK RABOLLI

CONYERS, GEORGIA

*This book is dedicated to the memory of **Jane Hurt Yarn** and **Jack Lindsay Falls**. They represented the breadth of the diverse membership of the 58,000-member Georgia Wildlife Federation. Each illustrated their love for the outdoors in very different ways, but they had something very important in common - they were devoted to the conservation of all wildlife and the habitat upon which it depends.*

Jane spent most of her adult life working within our political system making the protection of natural resources happen. She inspired, trained, and educated individuals, founded organizations, and worked to create the political will where none existed to benefit conservation. At age 71, she lost her long fight with cancer on October 18, 1995.

Jack spent his youth learning outdoor skills with his family and his camping, hunting and fishing companions. As a young adult, he developed a serious conservation ethic and he volunteered his time and energy to the conservation programs of the Georgia Wildlife Federation as an expression of his conservation ethic. At age 31, he lost his life in a construction accident on May 20, 1995.

On the cover: Cypress trees and alligators are popular sites in the Okefenokee National Wildlife Refuge in Georgia. Photos by Richard T. Bryant. Inset is the yellow-throated vireo, a neo-tropical migratory songbird, also found in the Okefenokee. Photo by Mike Hopiak, courtesy Cornell Laboratory of Ornithology.

On the back cover: Brasstown Bald, here dusted with snow, is the highest mountain in Georgia. Photo by Robb Helfrick. Top left: bobcats are found throughout the state. Photo by Richard T. Bryant. A painted bunting, a songbird found near coastal rivers. Photo by Karen Lawrence.

Copyright © 1996 by Georgia Wildlife Federation, Conyers, Georgia.

Design, typesetting by Lenz Design & Communications, Inc., Decatur, Georgia. 404-633-0501

Printed in the USA

Publisher's Cataloging in Publication
(prepared by Quality Books Inc.)

McCollum, Jerry.
    Georgia wildlife viewing guide / by Jerry McCollum, Betsie Rothermel, & Chuck Rabolli.
    p. cm.
    Includes bibliographical references.
    ISBN 0-9644522-1-9

    1. Wildlife viewing sites--Georgia--Guidebooks. 2. Wildlife watching--Georgia--Guidebooks. 3. Georgia--Guidebooks. I. Rothermel, Betsie. II. Rabolli, Chuck. III. Title.

QL171.M33 1996   508.758
                                QBI96-40150

ACKNOWLEDGMENTS

This book is a collective effort of many wildlife professionals, land managers, public and private organizations and agencies, dedicated amateur naturalists, and enthusiastic novices working together to create the most practical guide possible to viewing Georgia's wildlife. Sincere thanks are extended for the efforts of each one.

Specifically, our gratitude is due to the following persons who submitted viewing site nominations and drafted materials from which the editors worked: Steve Adam, Michelle Aldenderfer, Ken Akins, George Atnip, Greg Balkcom, Haven Barnhill, Charles Barnes, Jerry Bearden, Paul Bradshaw, Beth Brown, James Burkhart, Danny Burt, David Carlock, Hal Chestnutt, John Cissell, Bill Cooper, Bill Couch, Kevin Dallmier, William DeLoach, Daniel Drennen, Lane Eaton, Carlos Echevarria, Jim Ezell, Frank Ellis, Bill Fletcher, Dan Forster, Russell Garrison, Charlotte Gillis, David Gomez, Matt Griffin, Duane Harris, Mike Harris, Fred Hay, Dottie Head, Tom Hicks, Jerry Hightower, Tip Hon, John Jordan, Kent Kammermeyer, James Kendrick, Cliff Kevill, Guy LaChine, Susan Lampert, Angie Loggins, Scott McDonald, Mark McMillan, Patricia Metz, Lee Moon, Vince Mudrak, Nick Nicholson, Jim Nix, John Pafford, Jane Polansky, Carolyn Rogers, Bruce Roper, Steve Ruckel, Susan Shipman, William Tanner, Vince Taylor, Bill Tinley, Chuck Waters, Greg Waters, Charles West, Keith Whitaker, Bill Williams, E.J. Williams, Brad Winn, Wallace Woods, and Barb Zoodsma.

For their work as editors of specific sections or subjects of the book, our appreciation to: Jennifer Anderson and Terry Tatum.

Special gratitude is due to organizations and their leadership who supported the concept of a Georgia Wildlife Viewing Guide to be written and published in Georgia:

Georgia Department of Natural Resources, Lonice Barrett
 David Waller, Wildlife Resources Division Director
 Larry McSwain, Wildlife Resources Division Assistant Director
 Duane Harris, Coastal Resources Division Director
 Burt Weerts, Parks and Historic Sites Division Director
U.S. Forest Service Southeast Region
 George Martin, Forest Supervisor
National Park Service Southeast Region
 Robert M. Baker, Director
 Pat Stanek, Public Affairs
U.S. Fish and Wildlife Service Southeast Region
 Noreen Clough, Director
 Vicki Boatwright, Diana Hawkins, Public Affairs
 Bob Gasaway, Federal Aid
Georgia Power Company
 Mickey Brown, Land Department
 Don Still, Environmental Affairs
Ducks Unlimited, Inc. Dudley Ottley, MARSH Project Chairman

Thanks to the Georgia Wildlife Federation volunteers and staff who did a fabulous job typing some very rough original manuscript and checking facts, including F.G. Courtney, Gloria Eidson, Linda Henis, Maria Moreno, Jane Nave, Martha White, and Jim Wilson.

TABLE OF CONTENTS

TABLE OF CONTENTS

TABLE OF CONTENTS

THE AUTHORS

Jerry L. McCollum

A native of the north Georgia mountains, McCollum has spent most of his life studying and watching wildlife. He earned his AB and Masters Degrees from West Georgia College, before serving more than 15 years as a Wildlife Biologist with the Georgia Department of Natural Resources. He currently serves as President and Chief Executive Officer of the Georgia Wildlife Federation.

From left: Betsie Rothermel, Jerry McCollum, and Charles Rabolli.

Betsie B. Rothermel

A graduate of Cornell University's Natural Resources program, she earned her Master's degree in Ecology and Conservation Biology from The Pennsylvania State University in 1994. Prior to joining the staff of the Georgia Wildlife Federation, she worked in environmental consulting and, most recently, with the Nature Conservancy of Georgia.

Charles V. Rabolli

After graduating from The Pennsylvania State University with a Bachelor's degree in Forest Science, he continued his training at Clemson University in South Carolina, earning a Master's degree in Forest Science and Wildlife Biology. For 10 years he served as a Wildlife Biologist with the Georgia Department of Natural Resources. In 1992, he started an environmental consulting firm in Atlanta, Georgia.

TRAVEL REGIONS AND WILDLIFE VIEWING SITES

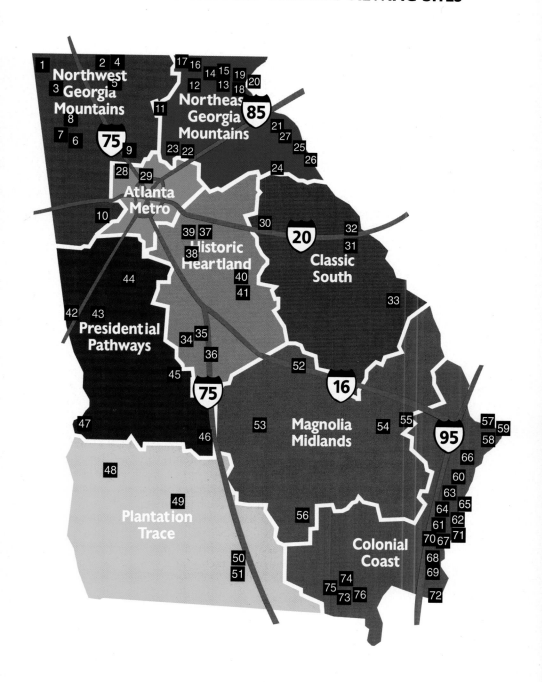

FOREWORD

Some of the most exciting times of my life have been those when I was watching wildlife. There is a feeling of accomplishment to be had from gaining access to the private lives of the native plants and animals with which we share the world. In fact, that accomplishment is greatly enhanced if we can enter and leave that special secret part of our world without being detected and without any disturbance to those wonderful objects of our fascination. This book is intended to help each person who uses it begin his or her own personal study of our native Georgia wildlife in a way that is safe for the person and safe for the wildlife, thus providing a rewarding experience which can become the foundation for understanding the need to protect our diverse wildlife community.

I remember as a small child being attracted to the movement of the natural world, a butterfly fluttering across the yard, a worm retreating into the ground as I turned up the dirt in my grandmother's garden, or a salamander darting away as I lifted a rock in the creek near the house. My fascination was, I now know, just the beginning of the process I would follow to learn and begin to understand the role these natural creatures played in the life of my own family.

Indeed, for a time I knew the earth worm and the salamander (then spring lizards) only as fish bait. And for a young fishing enthusiast, that gave these critters a high value for being. It was some time later when I learned from family members, renowned for living off the land, that the presence of the slimy earth worm was one of the key indicators that the soil in which our vegetables were produced was fertile and nontoxic. Similarly, I learned that those salamanders in the spring which provided our drinking water were so sensitive to their environment they provided a perfect early warning when there was a serious water quality problem with the family spring.

There are many beautiful, entertaining, and interesting pieces of the natural world to watch, and one of those pieces is our native wildlife. It is not always apparent that a particular species of wildlife performs a crucial service to mankind. There are perhaps many forms of wildlife which will not play a role in our survival on the planet. The question is, can we admire the butterfly simply for her beauty, taking as a matter of faith that she has a purpose for being? If that is enough for you to begin your journey using this wildlife viewing guide, then those of us who prepared the guide can have the faith that you will move to more complex observations which will cause us all, in the end, to protect all wildlife though its critical purpose is not revealed. Happy wildlife viewing.

Jerry L. McCollum
Certified Wildlife Biologist

FOREWORD

From the breathtaking mountains and rivers of her northern borders and the gently rolling Piedmont, to the fertile plains and the scenic marshes along her coast, Georgia boasts a rich diversity of scenery and habitat. This grand heritage is documented on the following pages by 76 of the innumerable sites in Georgia at which wildlife abounds. The observant visitor to one of these sites

David Waller

may see both game and nongame (non-harvested) species, of the furred, feathered, or scaled variety! The thrill of seeing these individual creatures will be second only to the thorough enjoyment of experiencing nature in its entirety.

Jim Fowler, former co-host of television's Wild Kingdom and one of today's foremost conservation spokesmen, has stated that one of the greatest threats to wildlife today is the insulation of humans from the natural world. As demands on out time and pocketbook increase, mankind's interaction with nature has tended to become a packaged exercise, wrapped in many layers of planning and preparation and limited to a handful of multiple-choice options. It doesn't have to be.

The Georgia Department of Natural Resources is excited to join the Georgia Wildlife Federation in providing residents and visitors to our unique state a publication which accomplishes more than simply directing individuals to geographic locations. For veteran wildlife watchers, the Georgia Wildlife Viewing Guide is the tool you have been waiting for. For amateur observers, the Guide is an introduction to some of our state's most impressive natural resources. And it is an introduction to a new way of seeing the world around you.

A share of the proceeds of this publication will go to the Nongame-Endangered Wildlife Program of the Department's Wildlife Resources Division. Funded almost 70 percent by voluntary contributions, the Nongame Program conducts projects aimed at conserving and enhancing nongame species, including over 100 animals found on the Protected Species List. Through our efforts, the Wildlife Resources Division hopes to ensure that the wildlife found in our state today will be here tomorrow and forever for future generations to enjoy.

David Waller, Director

Georgia Department of Natural Resources
Wildlife Resources Division

PROJECT SPONSORS

U.S. Fish and Wildlife Service

The mission of the USFWS is to conserve, protect, and enhance the nation's fish and wildlife and their habitats for the continuing benefit of the American people. The agency is responsible for protection and recovery of endangered species; enforcement of federal wildlife laws; research; and administration of the national wildlife refuge system and national fish hatcheries.

National Park Service

The National Park Service is charged with administering the units of the National Park System in a manner that protects and conserves their natural and cultural resources for the enjoyment of present and future generations.

Georgia Department of Natural Resources

Part of the mission of the Georgia Department of Natural Resources is to promote and encourage the conservation and preservation of the State's natural and cultural resources. We are pleased to contribute to this valuable guide, which will promote wildlife conservation and outdoor recreation.

National Fish and Wildlife Foundation

Chartered by Congress to stimulate private giving to conservation, the foundation is an independent nonprofit organization. Using federally-funded challenge grants, it forges partnerships between the public and private sectors to conserve the nation's fish, wildlife, and plants.

Georgia Power Company

The Georgia Power Company is proud to support the publication of the Georgia Wildlife Viewing Guide. The company also provides access to many Georgia Power Company lands and lakes for public recreation. For information about public access opportunities, call 1-800-846-4612, or visit the company home page on the Internet.

U.S. Forest Service, Department of Agriculture

The U.S. Forest Service has a mandate to protect, improve, and wisely use the nation's forest and range resources for multiple purposes to benefit all Americans. Georgia's national forests, the Chattahoochee and Oconee, contain 863,000 acres, and are home to many species of wildlife.

Ducks Unlimited MARSH Project

Ducks Unlimited, Inc. is a nationwide member organization which has protected millions of acres of wildlife habitat through its financial support of waterfowl habitat conservation and restoration. The development of its M.A.R.S.H Project (Matching Aid to Restore State Habitats) has also created some of the best wildlife viewing sites in the nation. A number of Georgia's M.A.R.S.H. Projects are included in this book. All are outstanding wildlife habitats.

Georgia Wildlife Federation

The Georgia Wildlife Federation is proud to sponsor this viewing guide as part of its mission to educate the public regarding the spectacular wildlife native to our state.

SUPERLATIVE SITES

If your time is limited for wildlife viewing in Georgia, you might want to check out these superlative sites.

HELPFUL TECHNIQUES FOR WILDLIFE VIEWING

This guide has been designed to afford the maximum opportunity to see and learn about Georgia's wildlife. A little advance preparation can greatly enhance your wildlife viewing experience. The viewing sites described are only a representative sample of the outstanding opportunities that exist across the State. Generally, these are sites that are open to the public, accessible without extraordinary effort, and offer a reasonably good chance of seeing the wildlife described. On a given day, however, some of these conditions may work against a successful wildlife viewing experience. Don't be quick to be disappointed. That's how the study of nature is — unpredictable. Remember to use the information presented here only as a guide to be added to the personal techniques you develop over time.

You don't have to be an expert, but it helps to know your subject in advance. As any field biologist will relate, luck often plays a significant role in spotting wildlife. You can greatly improve your chances of being in the right place at the right time, however, by understanding a little about the daily activity patterns and biology of the animals you wish to see. Find out if the animals are:

- primarily aquatic or terrestrial
- active during the day (diurnal) or at night (nocturnal)
- year-round residents or migratory visitors
- hibernating or nonhibernating
- abundant or very rare?

Field guides to birds, mammals, reptiles and amphibians, insects, and other animal groups, as well as those for tracks, nests, and food habitats, contain answers to these kinds of questions. Most bookstores and libraries carry such references, which typically provide maps showing the approximate distribution of each animal and describe the habitats in which it can be found.

BIRDS

Some birds are migratory, spending only part of the year in Georgia. Early morning is when birds tend to be most active. If you're not a morning person, you can still observe owls and other nocturnal birds. The distinctive calls and songs of many birds are often the best way to locate and identify them. Some species perform most of their daily activity in or near wetlands, others in open meadows, and still others deep in the forest interior. Noting the kind of habitat a bird is using may also provide clues to its identity, particularly for birds that occur in a limited range of habitats.

MAMMALS

As a rule, few mammals will be spotted in midday. Some species, like white-tailed deer and cottontail rabbits, are most active at dawn and dusk, but many more are nocturnal. By looking closely, you can detect abundant evidence of their night-time activities, such as browsed twigs, gnawed branches or tree trunks, piles of droppings, tracks, and nests.

REPTILES AND AMPHIBIANS

Like mammals, most reptiles and amphibians leave their daytime hiding places and resume feeding and other activities under the cover of darkness. You may be

Cottontail rabbits are often seen browsing on roadsides in early morning or evening.

able to locate some of these animals by driving slowly along less-traveled roads at night, particularly on warm nights with some precipitation when animals may be crossing the road. Reptiles you may see during the day include lizards, skinks, and water snakes or aquatic turtles basking on logs along rivers or in swamps. Many amphibians appear above-ground only a few weeks out of the year to breed, adding to our perception of them as rare. Often they are not as rare as appearances suggest, but they tend to be out on rainy nights when few people are outdoors. Most amphibians require moist environments and many spend part of their life cycle in the water.

INSECTS

Insects are scarce in winter, which is fortunate if you're visiting a site that supports a large mosquito population, but not if you are looking for moths and butterflies, most of which pass the winter in inactive pupal stages. Many insects begin life in an interesting aquatic stage before transforming into a dragonfly, stonefly, or other winged adult.

OUTFITTING YOURSELF FOR A WILD TIME

By paying attention to local weather reports, you won't be unpleasantly surprised by sudden changes in temperature or precipitation. Bring a change of clothes in case of rain or if there's a good chance you might get muddy and wet. Because of Georgia's large size and diverse environments, climatic conditions can vary greatly among geographic regions of the State. Waterproof footwear and a rain poncho can keep you out in the woods while others are running for their vehicles, preserving your camera and other equipment at the same time.

Certain tools will enable you to get a closer and better look at the wildlife you encounter. Binoculars are a must, particularly for viewing and identifying birds and other animals that like to keep a healthy distance. Ornithologists often use spotting scopes, which are more cumbersome but offer fantastic viewing.

Many would-be photographers have missed their "shot of a lifetime" while fumbling with a camera carrying case or lens cap. Having your camera out and ready to shoot ensures you will be prepared to take advantage of unusual wildlife encounters. Carrying a small hand lens or magnifying glass may come in handy for observing details. Some field guides use small, barely distinguishable features to separate one species from another, assuming, of course, that your subject is in hand. See below for more words of caution regarding handling wild animals.

PROTECTING YOURSELF AND THE WILDLIFE

Lack of reasonable caution or unbridled enthusiasm by the wildlife viewer can present problems that diminish viewing opportunities and may create unsafe conditions for both the viewer and the wildlife. Understanding and applying some simple principles will help avoid such situations and enhance what may become a life-long memory or family adventure in the outdoors.

Have a plan. It is advisable not to venture out alone, particularly in isolated areas. Let others know your travel plans and schedule so you will be missed if something goes wrong, and so others will know where to begin looking for you.

Wildlife is just that. Part of the excitement of catching a glimpse of a wild turkey or coyote is that you are observing the activity of a shy creature that exists independently of our care. Although providing food and cover for wildlife in your backyard may be helpful to many species, feeding wildlife on publicly owned lands can seriously hinder efforts to manage wildlife populations in a scientific manner and can create problems for local managers and visitors. Habituating wildlife to the presence of humans greatly increases the chances of negative interactions that could result in injury to people, the animal, or both. Any animal acting in a way inconsistent with its normal behavior should be avoided, because of the likelihood of disease. For example, an adult raccoon walking about in the middle of the day could be carrying rabies and should not be approached.

Most wildlife is not a threat to us when properly respected. As more and more habitat for wildlife disappears, you can consider it a very fortunate event to encounter a large indigo snake or other unusual species while hiking. Countless snakes are killed on Georgia highways each year, but few people are bitten by snakes, and it is exceedingly rare for a snake bite to be fatal. Nonetheless, you should be familiar with the six venomous species found in Georgia – copperhead, cottonmouth, coral snake, eastern diamondback, timber and pygmy rattlesnakes – and give any of these you encounter a wide berth. If you or a companion is bitten, the best course of action is to 1) remain calm and minimize the victim's movement, 2) carry the victim, if possible, to the vehicle and proceed immediately to the nearest hospital, preferably calling in advance so they can prepare for treatment, and 3) immobilize the affected area. Drastic measures such as using suction or tourniquets are not recommended if you are within easy reach of a medical facility (i.e., within one hour). In some cases, venomous snakes inflict a "dry" bite, that is, one in which no venom is actually injected. Be familiar with these and other first aid techniques and keep a good first aid kit and manual with you in the field.

The best home for wildlife is its natural environment. Wildlife watchers should resist the desire to make a domestic pet of wild animals. In general, wildlife found in Georgia do not make good pets. Logic should tell us that an animal well-suited to a natural habitat will be ill-suited to our homes. There are several other very good reasons to resist the urge to bring home a lizard, snake, bird, a fawn, or other animal you encounter.

Nongame Species: It is unlawful to capture or kill nongame wildlife except fiddler crabs, coyotes, armadillos, groundhogs, beavers, starlings, English sparrows, pigeons, and venomous snakes. Rats, mice, frogs, freshwater crayfish, freshwater turtles, salamanders, and freshwater mussels may be captured except for the species on Georgia's Protected Species List. All others are protected by law, and it is **illegal** to hold them without a permit issued through the Georgia DNR, Wildlife Resources Division. These permits are granted for educational and scientific purposes only.

Endangered Species: Some nongame species have additional protection under state and federal laws. Because they are threatened with extinction, it is a punishable federal offense to harass, capture, or harm any animal listed as threatened or endangered. The U. S. Fish and Wildlife Service or the Georgia DNR, Wildlife Resources Division can provide a list of these species.

Game Species: Designated game animals may be taken under certain conditions. A hunter taking a game animal must first purchase a permit (license), and then must observe exact conditions, such as: a specific time of year, time of day, size, and number and sex of the animal; wearing specified clothing; using a specified type of firearm, with specified type, caliber, power, and composition of ammunition; and attending a course of training in hunter safety. "Wanton waste" is also illegal, so that a hunter may not shoot an animal without the intent to retrieve and utilize that animal.

Most "babies" are not abandoned. Even though it may appear that a young animal has been abandoned because you can't immediately locate an adult, this is not true in many cases. Female rabbits, for instance, return to nurse their young in the nest only a couple of times per day, which could give the impression that the young animals have been abandoned. It is also untrue that human scent will deter birds from caring for their young if placed back in the nest, so a fallen nestling should be returned to its nest if it can be done quickly and safely. Otherwise, the best policy is to leave it alone.

Another reason for leaving wildlife in their natural homes is the difficulty and expertise required to care for wild animals properly. They may easily become sick and die without the proper nutrition and medical care. A network of licensed wildlife rehabilitators exists throughout the State. These rehabilitators are qualified to receive injured and abandoned wildlife and return them to health, with the aim of releasing them back into the wild. Contact the Wildlife Resources Division or a local nature center for information on a rehabilitator in your area.

Respect the rights of others, human and non-human alike. When hiking, respect "no trespassing" signs and others' property. Likewise, respect the dens and nests of wildlife. Standing dead trees, rocks, and logs provide valuable cover and breeding sites for reptiles, amphibians, and cavity-nesting birds and mammals. Some species are particularly sensitive to human disturbance. For example, bats that hibernate in caves have a decreased chance of survival if they are awakened by the noise and activity of visitors to the cave. When aroused out of hibernation, bats consume the precious energy stores they need to survive the winter cold.

Violations of any Georgia wildlife law may be reported to Project TIP (Turn In Poachers, Inc.) at 1-800-241-4113.

SUGGESTED REFERENCES AND ADDITIONAL SOURCES OF INFORMATION

Public libraries and bookstores:

Brown, F. and N. Jones (eds.). 1991. *The Georgia Conservancy's Guide to the North Georgia Mountains.* 2nd Edition. Longstreet Press, Atlanta, Georgia.

Bull, J. and J. Farrand, Jr. 1995. *National Audubon Society Field Guide to North American Birds.* Alfred A. Knopf Inc., New York, New York.

Choate, J. R., J. K. Jones, Jr., and C. Jones. 1994. *Handbook of Mammals of the South-Central States.* Louisiana State University Press, Baton Rouge, Louisiana.

Conant, R. and J. T. Collins. 1991. *Peterson Field Guides: Reptiles and Amphibians, Eastern/Central North America.* Houghton Mifflin Co., Boston, Massachusetts.

Duncan, W. and L. E. Foote. 1975. *Wildflowers of the Southeastern United States.* University of Georgia Press, Athens, Georgia.

McKee, G. (ed.). 1993. *A Guide to the Georgia Coast.* 2nd Edition. The Georgia Conservancy. Longstreet Press, Atlanta, Georgia.

Murie, O. J. 1974. *The Peterson Field Guide Series: A Field Guide to Animal Tracks.* Houghton Mifflin Co., Boston, Massachusetts.

Newcomb, L. 1977. *Newcomb's Wildflower Guide.* Little, Brown, and Co., Boston, Massachusetts.

Petrides, G. A. 1988. *Peterson Field Guides: Eastern Trees.* Houghton Mifflin Co., Boston, Massachusetts.

Schoettle, H. E. Taylor. 1993. *A Naturalist's Guide to St. Simon's Island.* Watermarks Printing Company, St. Simon's Island, Georgia.

Wharton, C. H. 1978. *The Natural Environments of Georgia.* Bulletin 114. Georgia Department of Natural Resources, Environmental Protection Division, Georgia Geological Survey, Atlanta, Georgia.

Georgia DNR, Wildlife Resources Division: You may request lists of species that occur in Georgia and descriptions of particular species by calling 770-918-6416 (Wildlife Resources Division Information) or 912-994-1438 (Nongame-Endangered Wildlife Program).

U.S. Fish & Wildlife Service: You may request lists of federally threatened and endangered species and other information by calling 404-679-7319.

Yellow pages: By looking under "Environmental," "Nature Centers," and "Wildlife Management" in the telephone book, you can find out how to contact local wildlife organizations and nature centers in your area.

THE NATIONAL WATCHABLE WILDLIFE PROGRAM

Similar books from many other states are part of the Watchable Wildlife Program coordinated by Defenders of Wildlife in Washington, D.C.

HOW TO USE THIS GUIDE

This guide is organized according to travel regions, with sections representing each of nine geographic areas within the state (see Georgia Map, p. 7). At the beginning of each section, you will find a map of the travel region showing locations of all the sites in the book located in that region, which are then described in the following section. The brief site descriptions in this guide are intended to provide an introduction to the site's natural history and wildlife viewing opportunities. The descriptions also include detailed notes regarding how to get to the site, who manages the site, where to call for more information, on-site facilities, and other relevant information. The following symbols are used where appropriate for easy reference:

SYMBOLS

To assist in locating sites designated as wildlife viewing areas, the Wildlife Resources Division, Georgia DNR has begun placing signs along highways near these areas. Look for this sign associated with the sites mentioned in this book, or other designated wildlife viewing areas throughout the state.

Entry Fee	Parking	Restrooms	Picnic	Camping	Hiking
Lodging	Boat Ramp	Large Boats	Small Boats	Bicycling	Horse Trails

Restaurant

VISITING GEORGIA'S STATE PARKS

Reservations for all Georgia State Parks can be made by calling (770) 389-7275 (in state) or (800) 864-7275 (outside Georgia).

Northwest Georgia Mountains

The Ridge and Valley and Cumberland Plateau physiographic provinces comprise this corner of Georgia. It is characterized by sedimentary geologic formations, including the Cumberland Plateau, Chickamauga Valley, Armuchee Ridges, and the Great Valley, also known as the Coosa River Valley. These formations contain many reminders of our ancient past in the form of fossils, which are apparent along almost any roadside rock ledge. They were sealed in the sedimentary deposits as the ancient seas receded. Dramatic vistas from the rim above Cloudland Canyon, and in the cathedral-sized rooms in the limestone caves of Pigeon Mountain, establish the extremes of the natural character of the region. The wildlife, too, is remarkable in its variety. Restored to the area by modern wildlife management programs, the majestic golden eagle soars over the mountain named for the passenger pigeon, driven to extinction by relentless "market" hunting. In the Great Valley to the west, the venomous cottonmouth, which is normally found in the blackwater streams to the south, has survived as a coastal plain remnant for millions of years.

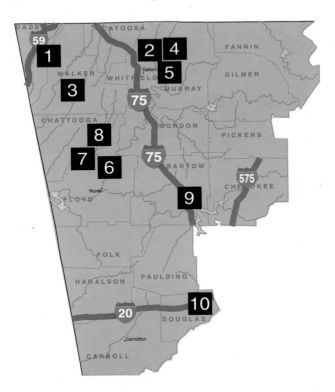

Right: Cloudland Canyon State Park

Cloudland Canyon State Park

Description: This viewing site is one of the largest and most scenic state parks in Georgia. The rugged beauty of the park is enjoyed year-round. Cloudland Canyon is an eroded gorge of nearly perpendicular slopes dropping 1,000 feet to the valley below. It is an excellent area to learn the fascinating geology which has formed the northeast corner of Georgia. Steep cliffs, open fields, hardwood forests, creeks, and mighty waterfalls are found throughout this natural treasure. An old farm now serves to demonstrate wildlife habitat management practices and attracts many species of game and nongame animals. Native fruiting vegetation and planted food plots bring wildlife in for a close view. Both easy and challenging hiking trails are available. The trails are well interpreted for lessons in both the natural history and geology of the area.

Viewing Information: A hillside platform overlooking planted food plots and ponds offers the best opportunities to see wildlife. One might see hawks, vultures, golden eagles, or peregrine falcons soaring overhead during fall migrations. There are also large populations of white-tailed deer and wild turkeys. Nearby Mc-Carty Bluff is the premier hang gliding site in the eastern U.S., providing a unique viewing opportunity for those who wish to watch others throw themselves off sheer cliffs.

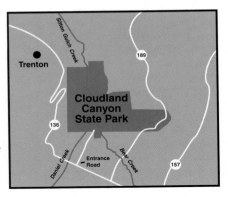

Directions: From Trenton, travel GA Hwy. 136 east 8 miles. Entrance is clearly marked.

Management: Georgia DNR, Parks and Historic Sites Division, 706-657-4050

Closest Town: Trenton, GA

Site Notes: observation platforms, cottages, interpretive programs (summer months), group shelter, group camp, picnic shelters, swimming pool, tennis courts

2 Lake Conasauga Recreation Area and Songbird Trail

Description: At 3,150 feet in elevation, Lake Conasauga is the highest lake in Georgia and the southern gateway to the awe-inspiring 34,000-acre Cohutta Wilderness Area. A hiker could not find a better area to explore than this wilderness. Nearly 90 miles of well-marked trails provide access to almost every habitat type in the Cohuttas. Lake Conasauga is a sparkling 19-acre lake with picnic areas, a boat ramp, a grass beach, and nearby camp grounds. Grassy Mountain, at 3,600 feet elevation, provides a beautiful backdrop to this alluring site. Three trails are accessible from the Recreation Area with travel through oak ridge forests, beaver ponds, grass fields, and cove forests.

Viewing Information: The three trails found here offer some of the best high mountain wildlife viewing in the State. Black bears, white-tailed deer, wild hogs, bobcats, raccoons, red and gray foxes, and mink are plentiful in the forests surrounding the lake and might be seen at any time

ISIDOR JEKLIN/CORNELL LABORATORY OF ORNITHOLOGY

The golden-winged warbler breeds in the Georgia mountains and winters in southern Mexico.

of the year. Around the lake look for kingfishers, wood ducks, and swallows. In the lake you might see bass, trout, or the shallow dish-shaped nests of bluegill. The tower at the end of Tower Trail is an excellent site for watching migrating vultures, hawks, and eagles in the spring and fall. The fall leaf color is also spectacular.

Songbird Trail is a 1.7-mile loop that passes through 300 acres of lands managed specifically to enhance songbird viewing by providing a diversity of habitats. Shrubs, forests, beaver ponds, and grassy areas each attract their own array of birds. Species seen here include chestnut-sided warblers, scarlet tanagers, rose-breasted grosbeaks, sandhill cranes, and red crossbills. An observation platform overlooking a beaver pond is an excellent place to observe wildlife. If you are going to the mountains to see wildlife, this is the place to go.

Directions: From Chatsworth, GA, travel north on US Hwy. 411 for apx. 4 miles. In Eton, turn right (east) at the traffic light onto old CCC Camp Road. Pavement ends after about 7 miles and then road becomes Forest Service Road 18. Travel about 4 miles and turn left (northeast) onto Forest Service Road 68. Continue on this road until you reach the main gate, about 10 miles.

Management: U. S. Forest Service, 706-695-6736

Closest Town: Chatsworth, GA

Additional Information: Weather can spoil the trip for those who are unprepared. Rain gear is recommended. Winter weather can be quite severe with temperatures below zero. Drinking water or a personal filtration system should be carried, as well as at least a one-day supply of food. There is a fee to camp at both camping facilities.

3 Crockford — Pigeon Mountain Wildlife Management Area

Description: This 13,000-acre area of great diversity and natural beauty offers a wide variety of wildlife viewing and recreation opportunities. Pigeon Mountain is the "thumb" of the broad, flat-topped Lookout/Pigeon mountain range. Driving on the top of this mountain feels like driving on a high table top where one is wary to approach the edges. Pigeon Mountain and Lookout Mountain drop off sharply in 1,000-foot escarpments offering breathtaking vistas of the valley below, known as McLemore Cove. The underlying limestone rock is laced with caves, accessible only to the most experienced cavers. The deepest cave pits in the eastern U.S. are found here. Rocktown

KAREN LAWRENCE

The juvenile, or eft, stage of the red-spotted newt is poisonous to potential predators.

Trail winds 1 mile through massive eroded boulders resembling three-story buildings and one which resembles a 25-foot-tall champagne glass. The Pocket Trail offers a combination of beautiful valley vistas, unusual eroded rock formations, and some of the prettiest and rarest spring wildflowers in the State. Pigeon Mountain was named for the extinct passenger pigeon which roosted on the mountain by the millions in the 1800s. The WMA was named in honor of Jack Crockford, the first professional wildlife biologist employed by the State of Georgia. Mr. Crockford invented and built the first "dart gun," a tool used today by wildlife professionals worldwide to capture wildlife safely.

Viewing Information: This is one of the few areas in the State where you may get a glimpse of the majestic golden eagle, made possible by a state reintroduction effort. Keep your eyes on the skies for many species of hawks and vultures soaring on the updrafts caused by the steep escarpments of the mountain. Green salamanders or the rare Pigeon Mountain salamander may be found by observant visitors. White-tailed deer and wild turkeys do well on this isolated flat mountain top. Spring and fall are filled with the calls and songs of migrating songbirds. Flora, fauna, geology, and scenic views — Pigeon Mountain has it all.

Directions: From LaFayette take GA Hwy. 193 west to Chamberlain Road. Turn left and go 3 miles to Rocky Lane Road. Turn right and go .5 miles to check station.

Management: Georgia DNR, Wildlife Resources Division 706-295-6041

Closest Town: LaFayette, GA

Site Notes: hunting, fishing, caving, rock climbing

P **⊞** **▲** **🚶** **🚲** **U**

4 Fort Mountain State Park

Description: Unique archeology, unexplained historic events, and a well-developed wildlife viewing area make this a rewarding adventure for the visitor with varied interests. The 3,200-acre park derives its name from an 855-foot-long stone wall on the top of the mountain. Why or by whom the wall was built remains unknown but theories abound. Expansive views to the east and west are magnificent from atop the 38-foot stone observation tower. One vista is of the Cohutta Wilderness Area. Visitors will enjoy the quiet beauty of 17-acre Fort Mountain Lake; the small stream leaving the lake cascades 400 feet down cliff faces, creating a sight and sound to behold. The .75-mile Big Rock Nature Trail showcases the rugged and diverse habitats found in the park. At the end of this trail is a wildlife viewing and demonstration area — both beautiful and educational. Over 14 miles of trails are incorporated into the park.

Viewing Information: This alluring park provides many wildlife viewing opportunities. Reptiles and amphibians are numerous around the lake edge, which is easily accessible by Lake Loop Trail. Beavers are a common sight for the quiet lake watcher. Bluebird boxes, bat boxes, seed feeders, hummingbird feeders, and special plantings make this area attractive to numerous species of wildlife. With the variety of offerings available, visitors may use binoculars to watch birds feed on seeds, or in the summer, hummingbirds at nectar feeders or cardinal flower, a native plant that thrives along moist stream banks. White-tailed deer, chipmunks, squirrels, black bears, bats, rabbits, and many other species inhabit and frequent the viewing area. **A special caution: do not feed the bears.** They are wild animals and should not be approached. Other interesting viewing opportunities include beavers, opossums, foxes, raccoons, and bobcats which roam through very early in the morning or late in the evening. Adding to the enjoyment of this wildlife viewing are interpretive signs that explain the simple requirements for developing a wildlife habitat in your own backyard.

Directions: Fort Mountain State Park is located 8 miles east of Chatsworth, GA on GA Hwy. 52.

Management: Georgia DNR, Parks and Historic Sites Division, 706-695-2621

Closest Town: Chatsworth, GA

Site Notes: interpretive programs, observation platforms, cottages

Additional Information: Visitors may stop at the park office for a free trail map and instructions for finding the wildlife viewing area.

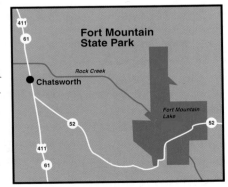

5 Coosawattee Wildlife Management Area

Description: This Wildlife Management Area has steep mountain slopes with ridgetop elevations of 1,600 feet and very narrow small stream valleys at around 700 feet in elevation. Visitors will want to travel the nature trail for excellent wildlife viewing opportunities. A boardwalk into a beaver pond provides a great chance for close-up views of beavers and their lodges. Rock outcrops and bluffs along the Coosawattee River and Talking Rock Creek are common. For canoeists, the beauty of the Coosawattee River above Carter's Lake should not be missed. Beautiful vistas from the river are best seen in April and October.

Viewing Information: Birds that are normally associated with wetlands may be seen along the nature trail. Great blue, green, and little blue herons and various species of puddle ducks may be seen. One record of a black-crowned night heron exists for the area. Many species of hawks use the area, and the majestic bald eagle is seen during most summers. During some years, osprey are common around Carter's Lake. Wild turkeys and white-tailed deer are numerous in the area. Other mammals that might be viewed by the patient observer include raccoons, opossums, minks, red and gray foxes, gray squirrels, and a host of other common small mammals. Carter's Dam, some 445 feet high, is the highest earthen dam east of the Mississippi River. Both black and turkey vultures normally roost on the high, exposed rock ledges adjacent to the dam.

Directions: From Chatsworth, travel south apx. 15 miles on Old Hwy. 411. Turn left into the recreational area as soon as you cross the Coosawattee River. The start of the nature trail is at the south parking lot of the recreation area at the Carter's Lake re-regulation Dam.

Management: Georgia DNR, Wildlife Resources Division, 706-295-6041

Closest Town: Chatsworth, GA

Additional Information: Restaurants and motels are available in nearby Chatsworth, Calhoun, or Ellijay, GA. Carter's Lake and Dam are adjacent to the nature trail site. There are two pay-to-use developed campgrounds and several free-use undeveloped campsites located around Carter's Lake.

6 Arrowhead Public Fishing Area and Wildlife Interpretive Trail

Description: Ready access, easy hiking, public fishing, natural history interpretation, wildlife habitat management demonstration, and abundant waterfowl make this area a "must-see" for the wildlife enthusiast. Fourteen ponds on this site are managed for waterfowl and public fishing. This wildlife oasis also offers a wildlife education center and a 2.2-mile wildlife interpretive trail. The 337-acre site contains a diverse mix of pine and hardwood forests, wildlife food plots, and wetlands, each with its own array of wildlife inhabitants.

Viewing Information: One of the best areas in the State to view Canada geese year round, Arrowhead PFA is also home to sig-

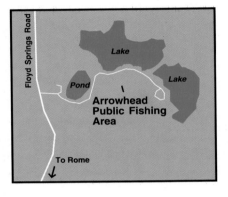

nificant numbers of migrating waterfowl, including mallards, scaup, teal, and ring-necked d ucks during fall and winter. And on a given winter day, you may see an amazing variety of other migrants. This is especially true 7-10 days after the severe winter weather begins in Canada and the northeastern U.S. Such events prompt reluctant migrant wildlife to leave for their southern destinations. Arrowhead provides good conditions for a short rest stop. Red and gray foxes, raccoons, mink, beavers, and white-tailed deer can be seen around the ponds and along the interpretive nature trail or from several observation platforms in the area.

Directions: From Rome take US Hwy. 27 north 9 miles to GA Hwy. 156. Turn right (east) and go 2.3 miles to Floyd Springs Road. Turn left and go 2 miles to the Arrowhead Regional DNR Office.

Management: Georgia DNR, Wildlife Resources Division, 706-295-6041

Closest Town: Rome, GA

Site Notes: observation platforms, interpretive hiking trail, public fishing area, Arrowhead Wildlife Education Facility

7 Rocky Mountain Public Fishing Area

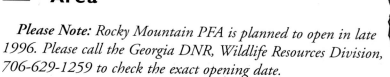

Please Note: Rocky Mountain PFA is planned to open in late 1996. Please call the Georgia DNR, Wildlife Resources Division, 706-629-1259 to check the exact opening date.

Description: Rocky Mountain PFA encompasses approximately 5,000 acres in the Ridge and Valley physiographic province of northwest Georgia. The area is part of a pumped-storage hydroelectric facility owned and operated by Oglethorpe Power Corporation. The habitats present include 600 acres of man-made impoundments, wetlands associated with the impoundments, predominantly hardwood forests, and palisades up to 1,400 feet in elevation that provide scenic overlooks of the valley below.

Viewing Information: Rocky Mountain PFA provides viewing opportunities for all species commonly found in hardwood forest habitats — white-tailed deer, wild turkeys, raccoons, opossums, gray squirrels, and others. All can be viewed at nearly any time of the day, but dawn and dusk are the best times for viewing. The impoundments and wetlands on the site attract waterfowl such as Canada geese, wood ducks, and mallards. Wading shorebirds such as egrets and various species of herons can also be seen. Fall and winter provide the best opportunity for viewing waterfowl and shore birds. Visitors are restricted to designated recreational areas of the project for safety reasons. Visitors should be able to enjoy wildlife in fairly close proximity due to the number of wildlife openings and associated overlooks that have been constructed. Access to the area is enhanced by a network of maintained trails and boat launching facilities.

Directions: From Rome, take US Hwy. 27 north apx. 10 miles. Turn west onto Floyd County Road 240 (Sike Storey Road) and proceed apx. 1 mile. Turn south on Floyd County Road 235 (Big Texas Valley Road). Continue apx. 7 miles to the site entrance on the left.

Management: Georgia DNR, Wildlife Resources Division, 706-629-1259

Closest Town: Rome, GA

Site Notes: observation platforms, interpretive programs, fishing jetties.

Additional Information: Rocky Mountain Public Fishing Area is adjacent to the Berry College Wildlife Management Area.

8 Berry College Wildlife Management Area

Description: A 30,000-acre mosaic of rural college campus, wildlife refuge, public hunting lands, and public fishing areas, the unique Berry College WMA contains virtually all of the habitats that occur in northwest Georgia — wide creek flood plains, open grassland, steep mountain slopes, reservoirs, old fields, wetlands, and mountaintop ridges. This diversity of habitats provides equally diverse opportunities for wildlife viewing. Elevation ranges from 600 feet at Victory Lake to almost 1500 feet along the ridge line of Lavender Mountain. Within this area is the Rocky Mountain PFA, 600 acres of impoundments managed for public fishing and wildlife viewing. Wildlife openings, scenic overlooks, nature trails, and boat ramps make this an area with diverse recreation opportunities.

KAREN LAWRENCE

Fall and winter are the best times to see wild turkeys, a common species on the Wildlife Management Area.

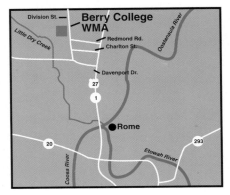

Viewing Information: The campus grounds and adjacent 5,000-acre wildlife refuge offer some of the best opportunities in the State for viewing wild turkeys and white-tailed deer. Turkeys and white-tailed deer venture into open fields at dusk and dawn with little concern for nearby humans. Fall and winter is the time to see these animals. The reservoirs attract wintering waterfowl and provide good viewing opportunities in a very scenic area. The forested mountain ridges are the southernmost mountain stop for many migrating songbirds. Excellent bird watching is available in fall and spring for warblers, vireos, hawks, and other migrating birds. A rare winter visitor to Georgia, the evening grosbeak was first seen in Georgia in this area in 1955. Look for small flocks of these striking birds feeding in winter on box elder, privet, and yellow poplar. They are easy to view while they are preoccupied with their feeding frenzy.

Directions: From Rome take US Hwy. 27 north to junction at Old Summerville Rd. Turn left on Old Summerville Rd. and go 1.5 miles to junction with CCC Road at check station.

Management: Georgia DNR, Wildlife Resources Division, 706-295-6041

Closest Town: Rome, GA

9 Red Top Mountain State Lodge Park

Description: Nearly 2,000 acres of mixed hardwood-pine forests on 12,000-acre Lake Allatoona, this park is a very scenic part of Georgia's Piedmont hill country. Scenic views of Lake Allatoona are available from the many trails throughout the park. This is a particularly beautiful spot for fall leaf color.

Viewing Information: Red Top Mountain is one of the best wildlife viewing sites within an hour's drive of downtown Atlanta. As with most of the State parks, wildlife is abundant and easily viewed. Roadside wildlife viewing areas and nature trails are managed specifically for wildlife viewing. Lakeside Trail is wheelchair accessible and is a demonstration area for attracting backyard wildlife. Bird feeders, nest boxes, wildlife plantings, and observation platforms are numerous throughout the park. White-tailed deer are abundant and readily observed. Ruby-throated hummingbirds and red-headed woodpeckers are also quite abundant. The miles of shoreline make it easy to find a quiet place to observe waterfowl and wading birds. This park is impressive year-round in both scenic beauty and wildlife viewing opportunities.

KAREN LAWRENCE

White-tailed deer fawns are a common sight during summer.

Directions: From Atlanta, travel north on I-75. Turn east at exit 123 and

29

travel 1.5 miles to the entrance.

Management: Georgia DNR, Parks and Historic Sites Division, 770-975-0055 (Lodge) or 770-975-4203 (Visitors Center)

Closest Town: Cartersville, GA

Site Notes: observation platforms, tours, hotel, interpretive programs, handicapped accessible trail, swimming beach, group shelters, conference rooms

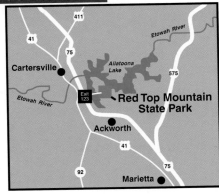

10 Sweetwater Creek State Conservation Park

Description: A wilderness experience only 15 miles from downtown Atlanta, here is an opportunity to see what the beautiful Piedmont of Georgia must have looked like 200 years ago before agriculture changed the landscape to what we see throughout much of North Georgia today. Hardwood forests of red oak, hickory, white oak, sweetgum, and yellow poplar dominate these beautiful rugged hills. Wildflowers abound. River cascades, rock outcrops, and steep cliffs are spectacular along Sweetwater Creek. Sweetwater Falls Overlook shouldn't be missed. This is also an interesting historic site, with ruins of a 19th century textile factory destroyed in the Civil War still evident.

Viewing Information: This wildlife oasis provides the

RICHARD T. BRYANT

Great blue herons fish along the banks of Sweetwater Creek.

Tracks of raccoons are often found near water where they hunt for crayfish and other prey.

best viewing opportunity anywhere near Atlanta. The 215-acre lake is home to hundreds of ducks and geese through the winter. Mallards, gadwalls, wood ducks, great blue herons and kingfishers are common sights. Beaver, fox, mink, and raccoon tracks are easy to find in the soft mud around beaver ponds. White-tailed deer are seen throughout the year in the food plots maintained for wildlife viewing and along the 6 miles of trails through the park.

Directions: From Atlanta, travel I-20 west to exit 12 (Thornton Rd./Camp Creek Pkwy.). Follow signs 2 miles to the park.

Management: Georgia DNR, Parks and Historic Sites Division, 770-732-5871 (Park Office)

Closest Town: Lithia Springs, GA

Site Notes: observation platforms, interpretive programs, 215-acre lake, bait and tackle shop, canoes, boat rentals

Additional Information: Stop at park office for a trail guide, then continue to trailhead parking area. Walking trails begin at this lot.

Northeast Georgia Mountains

This region is characterized by the metamorphic geology of the Southern Appalachians, an ancient mountain range originally formed by pressure, heat, and water that has been eroding for the past 400 million years. The resulting rounded mountain range has thus formed rich forest soils which support the most diverse plant life in the State, and in turn a highly diverse wildlife community. The wildflowers of the north-facing coves, such as Sosebee Cove, are world-famous. So, too, are the pure whitewater streams, as they leap over the falls of Tallulah, Amicalola, and Duke's Creek. The heaviest rainfall in Georgia occurs here, contributing to the lush green mountains and to the illusion of "smoke" with low-hanging clouds resting in the valleys many days during the year. The State's highest elevation (4784 feet) occurs here at Brasstown Bald. The 2000-mile-long Appalachian Trail begins here at Springer Mountain, creating a mythical, albeit man-made, connection to Mount Katahdin, the highest elevation in the State of Maine.

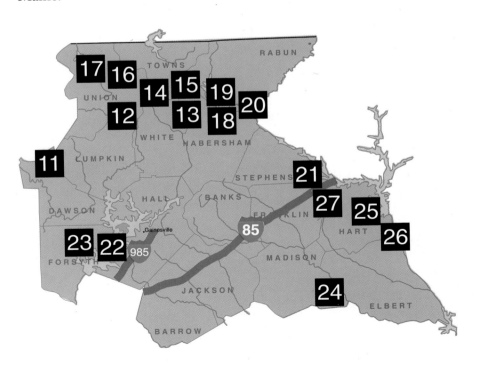

Right: Amicalol Falls.

▌▌ Amicalola Falls State Park/Dawson Forest Wildlife Management Area

Description: One of the "seven wonders" of Georgia, the park's breathtaking falls plunge 729 feet in seven cascades. Amicalola is the highest waterfall east of the Mississippi River. This stream flows through the park, offering visitors a chance to fish for trout. Consisting of more than 1,500 acres of beautiful mountainous habitat, the park is adjacent to the 741,000-acre Chattahoochee National Forest. The forest on the park is composed primarily of hardwoods, including southern

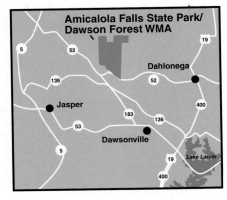

red oak, white oak, chestnut oak, sweetgum, sourwood, sycamore, maple, hickory, and yellow poplar, which are mixed with loblolly pine and Virginia pine. All seasons are beautiful at Amicalola, with an abundance of wildflowers in the spring and summer, such as dogwood, mountain laurel, and rhododendron. The fall season offers brilliant colors in the autumn forest. Winter months hold a special magic as white-tailed deer and other wildlife seek refuge within the park. Some visitors are fortunate to experience an occasional winter snow with accumulations of 2-10 inches which may not melt for up to a week. The park also offers

KAREN LAWRENCE

The colorful American kestrel is the smallest and most common falcon in Georgia.

many recreational opportunities including hiking, fishing, camping, and wildlife viewing. Amicalola offers an 8-mile approach trail to Springer Mountain, the southern terminus of the Appalachian Trail, and access to a mountain bike trail.

Viewing Information: Within the park, the forest offers nesting habitat for many species of warblers, vireos, and wrens. This beautiful river park is also home to squirrels, white-tailed deer, rabbits, raccoons, and bears. Wildlife can be viewed year-round and from most areas in the park. The higher elevations offer better viewing of raptors, vultures and, if you are lucky, an occasional osprey. Bluebirds, goldfinches, swallows, and sparrows are common park visitors in the winter and spring.

Directions: From Dawsonville follow GA Hwy. 53 west for 3 miles, turn right on GA Hwy. 183 and travel apx. 12 miles. Veer right onto GA Hwy. 52 and travel 2 miles. Amicalola Falls State Park entrance will be on the left.

Management: Georgia DNR, Wildlife Resources Division, 770-535-5700 (Dawson Forest), Georgia DNR, Parks and Historic Sites Division, 706-265-8888 (Amicalola Falls)

Closest Town: Dawsonville, GA

Site Notes: observation platforms, hotel, interpretive programs, 57-room lodge, 14 cottages, 17 campsites, comfort station, hiker shelter, visitors center (includes exhibits), gift shop, conference facilities, pioneer camping.

Additional Information: The visitors center contains several exhibits, one of which shows park guests how to attract wildlife to their backyards. The exhibit contains images of various mammals and birds native to this area. This exhibit continues to the exterior of the visitors center in a living exhibit.

Amicalola Creek flows through the beautiful Dawson Forest Wildlife Management Area just south of the park. Here a mosaic of diverse wildlife habitats offers additional wildlife viewing opportunities. The Amicalola Wildlife Interpretive Trail winds 3.5 miles along beautiful Amicalola Creek and is highlighted by a scenic view of the "Edge of the World" rapids, given a Class IV canoe rating.

Visitors should be cautious in winter months as snow and ice in this area of the State often make driving dangerous.

12 Woody Gap

Description: A picturesque mountain ridge gap where the Appalachian Trail crosses GA Hwy. 60, Woody Gap offers breathtaking scenery and recreational opportunities. From an elevation of 3,000 feet, scenic vistas of Yahoola Valley below make this a worthwhile and easily accessible stop on a leisurely drive through the mountains of North Georgia. The harsh ridge top environment is evidenced by wind-stunted and twisted oak trees along the Trail. An easy 1-mile hike on the Appalachian Trail, either north or south, offers scenic vistas and outstanding displays of spring wildflowers. Nearby Chestatee Overlook and Dockery Lake are "must-sees" while in this area.

Viewing Information: Woody Gap has excellent bird-watching opportunities, especially during spring migration. Early morning provides the best opportunity to see and hear numerous breeding songbirds, such as hooded warblers, black and white warblers, black-throated blue warblers, black-throated green warblers, as well as migrants, such as Cape May, blackpoll, and blackburnian warblers on their way to breeding grounds north of Georgia. These and numerous other species can be found on a short walk on the Appalachian Trail. Around the parking area, chestnut-sided warblers and indigo buntings are numerous. Longer walks along the trail may reward wildlife viewers with the drumming or explosive flush of a ruffed grouse. Wild turkeys are residents of this area and the surrounding National Forest, as are black bears and white-tailed deer.

Directions: From Dahlonega, take GA Hwy. 60 north apx. 17 miles. Woody Gap is well marked, with a parking area on the right.

Management: U.S. Forest Service, Gainesville Office, 770-536-0541

Closest Town: Dahlonega, GA

13 Dukes Creek - Smithgall Woods Conservation Area

Description: This 4,500-acre Conservation Area is a peaceful sanctuary for both people and wildlife. Once a privately-owned retreat from the hustle of modern living, this area is now owned and managed by the State with the same conservation objectives in mind. Access is limited to foot-traffic only and scheduled shuttle-bus tours. Easy hiking is available on the road system and several short interpretive trails. A mosaic of diverse habi-

Bird-foot violet, one of Georgia's most beautiful woodland wildflowers, blooms from March to June at Smithgall Woods.

tats offers many wildlife viewing opportunities. Hardwood forests, open fields, wildlife food plots, beaver ponds, and narrow stream valleys are all managed to provide a diversity of wildlife and recreation opportunities. Picturesque Dukes Creek winds and falls through the area and provides some of the best trophy trout fishing in the State. Picnic shelters throughout the site provide a place to relax with a lunch or escape a spring shower.

Viewing Information: Wildlife is abundant throughout the area. White-tailed deer, wild turkeys, squirrels, hawks and mountain songbirds are common sights. Beavers, herons, red-winged blackbirds and eastern bluebirds can also be seen. Observation blinds overlooking wildlife food plots are excellent spots for viewing and photographing wildlife. The keen eye has a chance of spotting trout resting in the calm waters behind creek boulders.

Directions: From Helen travel GA Hwy. 75 north for 1.5 miles. Turn left on GA Hwy. 356/Alternate 75 and travel 2.2 miles to entrance on left.

Management: Georgia DNR, Parks and Historic Sites Division, 706-878-3087

Closest Town: Helen, GA

Additional Information: This site is open to the public on Wed., Sat., and Sun. only. Trout fishing and tour bus by reservation only (706-878-3087). Nearby sites to visit include Unicoi State Park, Raven Cliffs Wilderness Area, and Dukes Creek Falls.

14 Raven Cliffs Wilderness Area

Description: Raven Cliffs Wilderness Area is in the Blue Ridge physiographic region. This 9,600-acre area is forested with a mature hardwood, white pine, and hemlock overstory on the slopes and ridges. The understory consists mostly of a Southern Appalachian evergreen community with mountain laurel, rhododendron, dog hobble, and galax. A beautiful mountain trail, Raven Cliffs Trail winds 2.5 miles up Dodd Creek to the base of 100-foot sheer cliffs. The trail generally follows the stream, and although it moves away from the streamside several times, you are never out of hearing of the tumbling whitewater. In late June, the luxuriant growths of laurel turn the stream borders into narrow swaths of white. The trail forks near the falls, and the right fork of the trail continues to the top of the cliffs. There is spectacular scenery from this pinnacle.

Viewing Information: Within the Raven Cliffs Wilderness Area and particularly along Raven Cliffs Trail are many good wildlife viewing opportunities. Listen for the guttural croaking of the common raven for which this area was named. This is one of the few areas in the State in which this bird can be found. Other high-elevation breeding birds that can be seen include the veery, solitary vireo, black-throated blue warbler, and rose-breasted grosbeak. The lucky visitor might glimpse the red squirrel or the New England cottontail rabbit, both rare in Georgia. White-tailed deer, ruffed grouse, wild turkeys and many migratory songbirds can be seen year-round.

Directions: Take GA Hwy. 75 north from Helen for 1.5 miles. Turn left on GA Hwy. 356/Alternate 75, and go 2.3 miles. Turn right on Richard Russell Scenic Hwy. and travel 2.8 miles to the trailhead and parking area.

Management: U.S. Forest Service, 706-754-6221

Closest Town: Helen, GA

15 Anna Ruby Falls and Scenic Area

Description: Anna Ruby Falls is the "poster" site for the clean, clear mountain streams of the Chattahoochee National Forest. This area is well-known for the thundering rush of double waterfalls crashing over rocky cliffs. Curtis Creek drops 153 feet and York Creek 50 feet to form the twin waterfalls known as Anna Ruby Falls. Easy access to the falls draws many visitors to this natural wonder. From the parking lot, a short paved footpath leads to the base of the postcard pretty falls. Walking this trail is easy and will take approximately 30 minutes. The 4.6-mile Smith Creek Trail is more of a challenge. This longer trail leads from the base of Anna Ruby Falls to nearby Unicoi State Park. Colonel John H. Nichols, who owned the falls after the Civil War, named the twin waterfalls in honor of his daughter Anna Ruby.

Viewing Information: Anna Ruby Falls Scenic Area, the 1600 acres surrounding the Falls, is a typical Appalachian Mountain plant and animal community with a profusion of flowering native perennials especially visible in the spring. Shrubs like mountain laurel and rhododendron are also abundant. Hiking along Smith Creek Trail, you might see white-tailed deer, gray squirrels, wild turkeys or even black bears. Many salamanders inhabit the numerous rocky creek bottoms crossed by the trail. Listen for warblers, vireos, and wrens as well. From the viewing deck of the visitors center, you can look down into Smith Creek and feed brook, rainbow, and brown trout. Anna Ruby Falls Recreation Area is open year round from 9:00 a.m. to dusk.

Directions: From Helen, travel north on GA Hwy. 75 for 1 mile. Turn right on GA Hwy. 356, travel 1.5 miles and follow signs.

Management: U.S. Forest Service 706-878-3547, Anna Ruby Falls Visitors Center 706-754-6221.

Closest Town: Helen, GA

Site Notes: observation platforms, snack machines, picnic sites with tables and grills.

Additional Information: Call U.S. Forest Service for more information and for an interpretive brochure from which the information in this site description was adapted.

16 Brasstown Bald and Wilderness Area

Description: At an elevation of 4,784 feet above sea level, Brasstown Bald is Georgia's highest mountain. The surrounding area is the 11,000-acre Brasstown Wilderness which provides habitat for a wide variety of plants and animals specially suited to cold, harsh environments and solitude from humans. For the hearty visitor this rugged area offers plenty of wilderness and wildlife viewing opportunities. A short but steep paved trail leads from the parking lot to the visitor information center on the Bald, which offers exhibits and interpretive programs.

A young gray squirrel explores its environment.

RICHARD T. BRYANT

Viewing Information: Birds that prefer high altitudes abound in spring and fall. The rose-breasted grosbeak, for example, prefers elevations above 3,000 feet and can be seen in good numbers in the rhododendron thickets along the trail to the Bald. Here in the spring may also be seen the black and white warbler, black-throated green warbler, veery, and winter wren. The area supports a large black bear population; white-tailed deer, ruffed grouse, and wild turkeys may also be seen. Exceptional spring wildflowers and fall color abound throughout the Wilderness Area and Bald. Visitors have access to four hiking trails up to 6 miles in length.

Directions: From Blairsville take U.S. Hwy. 19/GA Hwy. 129 south for 8 miles. Turn left (east) on GA Hwy. 180, go 9 miles to GA Hwy. 180 Spur. Turn north and go 3 miles to parking lot.

Management: U.S. Forest Service 706-896-2556, Brasstown Bald Visitors Center 706-745-6928.

Closest Town: Blairsville, GA

Site Notes: observation platforms, interpretive programs, bookstore, shuttle bus

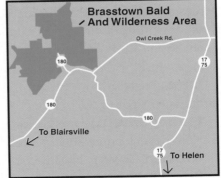

Brasstown Bald
And Wilderness Area
Owl Creek Rd.
180
17 75
180
180
To Blairsville
17 75 To Helen

17 Sosebee Cove Scenic Area

Description: A beautiful high-elevation north-facing cove with unique flora and fauna, this easily accessible site will inspire the visitor with its huge buckeyes and tulip trees. Other species characteristic of more northern latitudes include basswood, black birch, striped and mountain maple, and the rare yellow wood tree. Impressive boulder fields offer a profusion of spring wildflowers, mosses, and ferns. A loop trail through the cove makes for a rewarding trip.

Spring wildflowers like this large-flowered trillium are protected by law on public lands.

Viewing Information: Cove forests are known for their rich variety of salamanders. Here you will find the seal salamander, purple salamander, black-bellied salamander, and two-lined salamander. Creek chubs, river chubs, and saffron shiners make the cold-clear stream their home. Spring bird watching can be excellent. American redstarts, rose-breasted grosbeaks, Kentucky warblers, hooded warblers, and black and white warblers are common sites. White-tailed deer, black bears, and ruffed grouse also might be seen.

Directions: From Vogel State Park, travel north on US Hwy. 129 for about .25 miles. Turn left (west) on GA Hwy. 180 and travel 4-5 miles. Sosebee Cove is marked and loop trail begins on the right side of road.

Management: U.S. Forest Service, Brasstown Ranger District, 706-745-6929

Closest Town: Blairsville, GA

18 Moccasin Creek State Park and Burton Wildlife Management Area

Description: Opportunity abounds at this park and the surrounding rugged back country. A visitor could spend a week exploring the many diverse areas available by car alone. The park, located on magnificent Lake Burton, offers expanded opportunities to the visitor with a boat. Also located near the park is the Burton Fish Hatchery, offering the opportunity to see trout-rearing facilities and trout destined for stocking the streams of mountainous North Georgia. The rugged mountains rising to the west are part of the 12,800-acre Burton WMA offering access

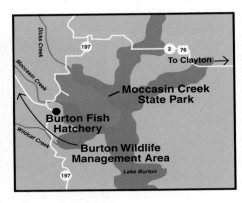

to the giant buckeyes of Ramp Cove, the gnarled ridgetop oaks of Keller Ridge, the rock outcrop of Mill Creek Rough, the Appalachian Trail, and the magnificent boulder fields of Tray Mountain.

Viewing Information: In winter, many surface-feeding and diving ducks visit the site, including buffleheads, ring-necked ducks, mergansers, mallards, Canada geese, blue-winged teal, American coots, and occasionally pintails. Canada geese are a common sight at the park. Along the nature trail you may see white-tailed deer, groundhogs, warblers, flycatchers, and an occasional black bear. Overhead, look for soaring hawks and osprey. The bald eagle is also an occasional winter visitor. Magnificent hiking trails are available, especially on the western portion of the management area. The mosaic of habitats provides superb displays of spring wildflowers.

Directions: Travel 20 miles north from Clarkesville, Georgia on GA Hwy. 197. Entrance is marked.

Management: Georgia DNR, Parks and Historic Sites Division, 706-947-3194. Burton WMA, Wildlife Resources Division, 770-535-5700

Closest Town: Clarkesville, GA

Site Notes: observation platforms, trails, interpretive programs

Right: Moccasin Creek in summer.

19 Lake Burton Fish Hatchery

Description: Lake Burton Fish Hatchery is located in a rural, mountainous area of Rabun County in extreme northeast Georgia. Elevation of the hatchery is approximately 1,920 feet above sea level. Lake Burton, a 2,700-acre Georgia Power Company lake, borders the facility on its eastern side, with the Chattahoochee National Forest forming the northern and western boundaries. Forest types include stands of oak, pine, hemlock, mountain laurel, and many other native mountain plants. The Appalachian Trail, snaking its way south to its beginning point at Springer Mountain and north toward North Carolina, follows the ridge line above the headwaters of Moccasin Creek, the water source for Lake Burton Hatchery.

Viewing Information: Lake Burton Fish Hatchery features a unique opportunity to view both birds and mammals and explore the habitat of animals that live in both cold and warm water. Several species of migrating ducks, including mallards and buffleheads, mergansers and loons can be seen during the fall and

RICHARD T. BRYANT

Brook trout, Georgia's only native trout, inhabit clear, cold mountain streams.

winter on Lake Burton and resting on the hatchery ponds. As winter gives way to spring, songbirds in their mating colors can be seen nesting in the surrounding forested areas. It is also possible to view hummingbirds feeding on colorful plants near the water and forest edges. An occasional osprey or bald eagle may be seen soaring over Lake Burton at any time. Kingfishers and both great blue and green herons stalk the shallow lake edge. While walking the nature trail from the hatchery or traveling Hemlock Trail up Moccasin Creek, you may encounter turkeys or white-tailed deer and small mammals such as squirrels, chipmunks, raccoons, and rabbits. If you are extremely lucky, you may encounter a black bear or at least view a bear track on a sand bar near the creek. During trout fishing season, you can fish Moccasin Creek for rainbow, brown, and brook trout. Brook trout are the only trout native to Georgia. Fishing piers along the edge of the lake offer an opportunity to view warm water fish such as bluegill, redbreast sunfish, largemouth bass, and yellow perch in their natural habitat. This geographical area is also a favorite stopover for the monarch butterfly during its annual migration in the spring and summer months.

You may also tour Lake Burton Hatchery to see rainbow and brown trout being raised for stocking into mountain streams in North Georgia. The hatchery is open daily from 8 a.m. until 4 p.m. for visitors to learn about trout, trout habitat, and aquatic life in cold and warm water habitats. Guided tours are also available year-round for organized groups. Reservations are required.

Directions: From Clarkesville, GA, take GA Hwy. 197 north for 20 miles. Entrance can be seen from the road.

Management: Georgia DNR, Wildlife Resources Division, 706-947-3112

Closest Town: Clarkesville, GA

Site Notes: tours, interpretive programs

Additional Information: The adjacent Moccasin Creek State Park offers numerous camping, recreation, and natural history interpretation opportunities. If you plan to hike the trails during the spring, be prepared for frequent rain showers. If you plan to camp during the winter, be prepared for temperatures which routinely fall below freezing.

20 Tallulah Gorge State Park

Description: One of Georgia's most spectacular natural wonders, this 800-foot-deep gorge is one of the steepest and most spectacular gorges in the East. Breathtaking views of the gorge against a backdrop of rugged mountains attract many visitors. The gorge is nearly 2 miles long and .5 miles wide. For the hardy hiker, several steep trails descend into the bottom of the gorge. Magnificent views into the gorge are available at rim overlooks and along trails into the gorge. The Tallulah River was dammed at the head of the gorge in 1913 and diverted to an electric generating plant. Thundering waters have only recently been restored to the gorge on a limited number of spring and fall weekends. Tallulah Falls Lake provides quiet serenity in contrast to the grandeur and power of the gorge.

Viewing Information: Best viewing opportunities are for cliff-inhabiting birds and amphibians. You might see swallows, swifts, and phoebes nesting in the crevices of the gorge walls. Look for hawks and vultures circling overhead. Amphibians are numerous in the moist cliff-face environment. The inquisitive visitor may see dusky salamanders, slimy salamanders or spotted salamanders. If lucky, you might spot the rare seepage salamander or green salamander. Very rare flora of the gorge includes Carolina hemlock and persistent trillium.

Directions: From Atlanta, take I-85 north to I-985 north to GA Hwy. 365. Take US 441 north to Tallulah Falls. Follow signs to the park entrance.

Management: Georgia DNR, Parks and Historic Sites Division 706-754-7979. Park Office 706-754-7970.

Closest Town: Tallulah Falls, GA

Site Notes: observation platforms, interpretive programs, swimming beach, 65-acre lake, and tennis courts.

Additional Information: Park facilities include the 16,000 sq. ft. Jane Hurt Yarn interpretive education center featuring exhibits on the historical, cultural, and natural science aspects of Tallulah Gorge. This center offers a unique bird watching station, various examinations of the unique ecosystems, and a 75-seat theater. Access to the gorge floor is by permit only.

21 Tugaloo State Park

Description: Four hundred secluded acres surrounded by scenic Lake Hartwell, Tugaloo State Park is forested with a diverse mix of oaks, hickories, and pines. The visitor with a boat has access to the 56,000 acres of Lake Hartwell. Three miles of easily accessible shoreline provide excellent opportunities for viewing waterfowl. An abundance of flowering dogwood, black cherry, and sweetgum provide large amounts of fall wildlife food.

Viewing Information: Waterfowl are numerous on Lake Hartwell in the fall and winter. Canada geese, ring-necked ducks, mallards, wood ducks, mergansers, common loons, and many other species of waterfowl frequent the area. An observation platform overlooks the lake from a nearby oak-hickory ridge. Several wildlife openings with observation platforms are also found on the park. White-tailed deer and wild turkeys are numerous on the park. Red foxes, gray foxes, raccoons, and hawks are common sights. Overhead, listen for the nasal call of the fish crow or the high rapid chirping of the bald eagle. The wildlife is plentiful and easily seen from the trails, roads, boat docks, and shoreline.

Directions: Take I-85 north to exit 58, GA Hwy 17. Follow park sign to the right onto County Road 385 (Garrard Road). Go 1.5 miles and turn left. Proceed 3.3 miles to Tugaloo State Park Road and turn right. Park is located at the end of the road. The Tugaloo State Park office is first building on left.

Management: Georgia DNR, Parks and Historic Sites Division, 706-356-4362 (Visitors Center) or 404-656-2770
U.S. Army Corps of Engineers Lake Hartwell 706-376-4788

Closest Town: Lavonia, GA

Site Notes: observation platforms, tours, cottages, interpretive programs, beach area, group shelter

22 Lake Lanier and Buford Dam

Description: This area includes a 38,000-acre lake with over 100 islands, 540 miles of shoreline, 10 marinas, 70 recreation areas and many miles of the Chestatee and Chattahoochee rivers located in the upper piedmont region of the State at the foothills of the Blue Ridge Mountains. Surrounding the lake are forests of southern red oak, hickory, sweetgum, tuliptree, loblolly pine and Virginia pine. During spring and summer the shorelines are a profusion of color provided by flowering dogwood, azalea, mountain laurel, rhododendron, and holly. Although this is the busiest recreation lake administered by the U.S. Corps of Engineers, it is easy to find a quiet spot for wildlife viewing on one of many islands or along the shore.

Viewing Information: With its burst of color and abundance of migrating songbirds, spring is the best time for wildlife viewing.

RICHARD T. BRYANT

Longear sunfish have been stocked in many Georgia lakes including Lake Lanier.

Look overhead for soaring bald eagles, which are regular visitors to the lake. Canada geese, great blue herons, green-backed herons, kingfishers and ospreys are common during the summer.

The forest surrounding the lake is a refuge for squirrels, rabbits, white-tailed deer, and wild turkeys. The Chattahoochee below Buford Dam offers an excellent opportunity for solitude and viewing elusive wildlife. Laurel Ridge Nature Trail winds 4 miles along the lake, dam and Chattahoochee River below the dam. Numerous viewing stations and interpreted points of interest are found on this trail. Many visitors come to the lake to fish for striped bass, largemouth bass, smallmouth bass, crappie, and trout.

Lake Lanier and Buford Dam

Chestatee River
Chattahoochee River
19
129
985
Lake Lanier
Gainesville
129
Buford Dam
985
85
400
Buford
Chattahoochee River
Exit 45

Directions: From Atlanta, follow I-85 north to I-985, then follow the signs.

Management: U.S. Army Corps of Engineers, 770-945-9531

Closest Town: Gainesville, GA

Site Notes: tours, interpretive programs

Additional Information: The Department of Natural Resources operates a trout hatchery near the dam where visitors can see and learn about trout and their habitats. Excellent trout fishing is available in the Chattahoochee River.

23 Buford Trout Hatchery

Description: Buford Trout Hatchery is located in the Chattahoochee River flood plain. The river bank is forested with walnut, birch, oak, and tulip poplar trees. The hatchery grounds include old fields and constructed raceways for rearing trout. Here is an excellent opportunity to see thousands of young rainbow, brook, and brown trout being raised for release into the trout streams of the North Georgia mountains.

Viewing Information: Although the hatchery is only 36 acres, it offers an opportunity to view a number of birds and mammals. Blue and green herons and kingfishers are relatively common in the morning or at dusk. Great egrets and ospreys can be seen as unexpected visitors. Hawks and vultures are common during the day. A variety of ducks fly along the river and can be seen frequently. Songbirds are common and can be viewed seasonally. Small mammals are not common, but beavers, mink, and otters can be viewed on occasion by the patient observer. White-tailed deer sometimes leave the surrounding woods and venture onto the hatchery grounds. The hatchery is open to visitors year-round during daylight hours.

Directions: From the intersection of GA Hwy. 400 and GA Hwy. 20 south of Cumming, go east 3.5 miles on GA Hwy. 20. Turn left on Pruitt Road and go .75 miles to Trout Place. Turn right to the hatchery. Access to the Chattahoochee River National Recreation Area is along the path that starts at the hatchery gate. Access to the hatchery is from the parking area inside the gate.

Management: Georgia DNR, Wildlife Resources Division, 770-781-6888

Closest Town: Cumming, GA

Additional Information: The hatchery staff will schedule tours for organized groups. Tours must be scheduled in advance. The emphasis of these tours is the trout hatchery and trout management.

24 Watson Mill Bridge State Park

Description: One thousand acres straddling the peaceful south fork of the Broad River, Watson Mill Bridge is one of Georgia's most scenic state parks. The river and historic covered bridge are the focal points of the park, but the park is also well-known for its natural history interpretive exhibits and abundant wildlife. Ponds, rivers, streams, beaver dams and associated wetlands, bottomland hardwood forests, steep banks, granite outcrops, and pine forests make up a mosaic of habitats in the park. An extensive trail system for both hikers and horseback riders makes all these habitats easily accessible. Wildlife is abundant, and the short drive from Athens is worth the trip.

A young river otter depends on the river that flows through the park.

Viewing Information: The quiet solitude of this park makes wildlife viewing particularly enjoyable. Bird watching is excellent year-round. The best area for bird watching is around the parking area at the beginning of the horse trail. Wild turkeys, white-tailed deer, and woodland songbirds are all easily seen along the horse trails. Canoes and paddle boats can be rented here for wildlife viewing from the beautiful south fork of the Broad River. A highlight of this site is the outstanding wildlife display at the park office. Here, diagrams featuring Georgia wildlife in natural habitats are both beautiful and educational. Start your wildlife viewing from here and then hit the trail!

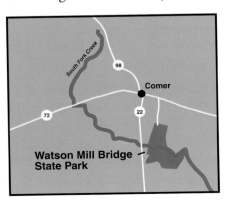

Directions: From Athens, take GA Hwy. 72 to Comer. From Comer follow the State park signs south on GA Hwy. 22 and turn left on Watson Mill Park Road. Entrance is marked.

Management: Georgia DNR, Parks and Historic Sites Division, 706-783-5349 (Visitors Center)

Closest Town: Comer, GA

25 Lake Richard B. Russell State Park

Description: One of Georgia's newest and, for now, least-known state parks, this nearly 3,000-acre park with over 7 miles of trails provides plenty of opportunities to find a quiet spot for uninterrupted wildlife viewing. Surrounded on three sides by Lake Russell, the park is an oasis for both humans and wildlife. The majority of the site is forests of oak, hickory, sweetgum, flowering dogwood, and black gum. Dense stands of redcedar have grown up in what were once cotton and tobacco fields. Open fields add to the diversity of habitats, and therefore the diversity of wildlife. Numerous small, protected coves are favorite spots for waterfowl, wading birds, and beavers.

Viewing Information: This protected site has become a refuge for large numbers of wildlife. White-tailed deer and turkey populations are very large and they are frequently seen. Downy woodpeckers, hairy woodpeckers, and red-bellied woodpeckers are common in these quiet woods. Canada geese, ducks, mergansers, and loons might be seen during the fall and the winter months. Rabbits, coyotes, foxes, raccoons, and opossums are best seen at dawn and dusk. The lake coves and adjacent small streams harbor snakes, turtles, and salamanders.

Directions: From Elberton, travel GA Hwy. 77 north 2 miles. Turn right on Ruckersville Road, and travel 7 miles to park entrance on the right.

Management: Georgia DNR, Parks and Historic Sites Division, 706-213-2045 (Visitors Center)

Closest Town: Elberton, GA

Site Notes: interpretive programs, rowing area and dock, historic structure

26 Bobby Brown State Park

Description: This beautiful lake park lies between the Broad River and Savannah River where they join to form Clark Hill Reservoir. Nearly surrounded by water, this park is a quiet refuge for humans and wildlife alike. This site was the location of the third largest town in Georgia during the early 1800s. Mixed forests of hardwoods and pine cover this peninsula and provide a home to a variety of wildflowers and wildlife. Two miles of trails offer plenty of wildlife viewing opportunities. Miles of lake shoreline are easily reached by the trail system and offer beautiful views of the surrounding rolling, forested hills.

Viewing Information: Cade Trail and History Trail have interpretive signs that provide natural history information on the plants and animals seen along the trail. Near the beaver ponds, look for raccoon, otter, and mink tracks in the soft mud. Mallards, blue-winged teal, wood ducks, and Canada geese often rest in the many coves along the shoreline. An elevated observation deck overlooks the confluence of the Broad and Savannah Rivers. Look overhead for bald eagles as these are a common sight during spring and summer. Large populations of white-tailed deer, wild turkeys, gray squirrels, and songbirds are found throughout the park. Along the lake edge, search the shallow waters for large-mouth bass, redear sunfish, and bluegill.

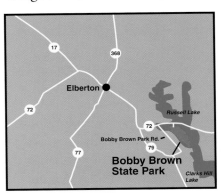

Directions: From Elberton, take GA Hwy. 72 east 14 miles to Bobby Brown State Park Road. Turn right onto park road and continue for 7 miles to the entrance.

Management: Georgia DNR, Parks and Historic Sites Division, 706-213-2046

Closest Town: Elberton, GA

Site Notes: showers, pioneer camping, swimming, annual special events

27 Victoria Bryant State Park

Description: A small park with surprising habitat diversity, Victoria Bryant State Park is located in the Upper Piedmont at the foothills of the mountains and displays mountain, Piedmont and Coastal Plain habitats. North-facing creek slopes exhibit mountain vegetation such as mountain laurel, galax, trilliums, and foam flower. Typical Piedmont trees dominate the site, including southern red oak, white oak, tulip tree, sourwood, and flowering dogwood. Large patches of switch cane, more commonly associated with Coastal Plain habitats, are found along Rice Creek. A half-mile scenic nature trail is excellently interpreted with a pamphlet. An elevated platform overlooking a granite outcrop is a great place for sitting quietly to observe wildlife. Perimeter Trail is wheelchair-accessible for 100 yards and includes one observation deck overlooking a 2-acre pond and a second observation deck overlooking a 4-acre wildlife food plot.

Viewing Information: Bird-watching opportunities abound along both trails. The diversity of habitats encountered along the trails enhances the opportunity to see a wide variety of birds and mammals. White-tailed deer and turkey tracks are numerous in the soft mud along the trails. From the observation deck overlooking the pond, look for Canada geese nesting on a small island or ducks and great blue herons feeding in the shallows. Look for bass and bream near the pond edges in the early spring. Wild turkeys, red and gray foxes, bobcats and white-tailed deer feed or hunt in the food plots visible from the observation deck. Midwinter might find small flocks of migrating woodcocks probing for worms in the switch cane patches.

Directions: From Franklin Springs, travel US Hwy. 29 northwest 1 mile. Turn right onto GA Hwy. 327, and travel 1 mile to the park entrance on the left.

Management: Georgia DNR, Parks and Historic Sites Division, 706-245-6270 (Visitors Center)

Closest Town: Franklin Springs, GA

Site Notes: observation platforms, interpretive programs, 9-hole regulation golf course, swimming pool, playgrounds

Atlanta Metro

    A progressive business boom town, the greater metropolitan Atlanta area is also the most heavily forested city in America. Stringently enforced ordinances help minimize the loss of the forest. Much of the understory of this urban forest is provided and maintained by the people of Atlanta, many of whom enjoy gardening as a serious hobby. There are, in fact, many residential gardens in Atlanta that are maintained specifically for wildlife. And through it all runs the Chattahoochee River, which forms a magnificent metropolitan wildlife corridor as it meanders through the heart of the city. On the north side of the city may be found a very good and equally rare trout fisher's dream, a metropolitan trout stream, which is only one superlative feature of the Chattahoochee National Recreation Area. To the east are located the fragile granite monoliths, Stone Mountain and Panola Mountain. On the south side is an ancient site of human occupation known as Soapstone Ridge, where bowls and other tools were carved from the stone of the area. Finally, to the west, Sweetwater Creek empties its sparkling tributary waters into the Chattahoochee.

28 Kennesaw Mountain National Battlefield Park

Description: For the visitor interested in Civil War history and wildlife viewing, this is the site to visit. Located in the foothills of the Appalachian Mountains, this 2,900-acre park is a patchwork of diverse habitats providing many wildlife viewing opportunities. Pine forests, mixed hardwood-pine forests, open fields, wetlands, mountain tops, and creek bottoms are each easily accessible and abundant in wildlife. Roadside and trailside exhibits, earthworks, and battlefield structures tell the story of the 1864 Atlanta Campaign of the Civil War. An extensive trail system through a variety of habitats makes this an excellent bird watching area.

Viewing Information: This site provides outstanding opportunities for viewing songbirds. Kennesaw Mountain offers good bird watching and excellent mountaintop vistas year-round from its 1800-foot peak. The mountain is a regular stop for migratory songbirds during both spring and fall. The mowed battlefields and adjacent wooded edges are favored by tree sparrows, field sparrows, white-throated sparrows, song sparrows, and eastern bluebirds. Turkeys, foxes and white-tailed deer also venture into the fields at dusk and dawn. Beavers, herons, and blackbirds can be seen at beaver ponds along several creeks on the site.

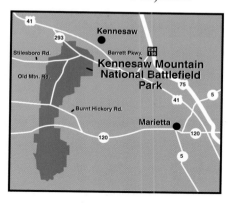

Directions: From Marietta, travel north on I-75 to exit 116 (Barrett Parkway), turn west on Barrett and travel apx. 1.5 miles. Turn north on US Hwy. 41 (Cobb Parkway), go to second light and turn left onto GA Hwy. 293. Travel 3 miles to first intersection inside the park, and turn right on Stilesboro Road. Visitors center and parking on left.

Management: National Park Service, 770-427-4686

Closest Town: Marietta, GA

Site Notes: observation platforms, civil war museum

29 Chattahoochee River National Recreation Area

Description: The Chattahoochee River National Recreation Area consists of 48 miles of Upper Piedmont river and 14 separate land units along the river. The 4,200 acres in the land units provide a rich mosaic of river corridor habitats: steep ravines, hardwood forests, river flood plains, and meadows, each with its own array of wildlife. The river corridor is a linear extension of a more northern mountain-type environment. A surprisingly wild and scenic refuge for humans and wildlife alike in an otherwise urban area, this river park is a place rich in natural and human history.

Viewing Information: Despite being surrounded by urban and suburban development, Chattahoochee River NRA is a wildlife viewing opportunity not to be missed. It is the southernmost habitat for many animal and plant species that are normally found in the mountains. Many of the ravines along the river contain attractive tributary streams and support unique vegetation almost undisturbed by man. Beaver ponds dot the Recreation Area and provide a year-round haven for wood ducks, muskrats, minks, and beavers. Winter visitors include mallards, black ducks, Canada geese, and the occasional pintail. The undisturbed riverbank

ROBB HELFRICK

Wildlife sightings are likely during early morning strolls along the river.

Wood ducks are common cavity-nesting birds along the river.

forests are home to large populations of white-tailed deer, wild turkeys, and red and gray foxes. River otters, cottontail and swamp rabbits, chipmunks, and squirrels can also be seen here. Great blue herons are extremely common, and in the fall great numbers of vultures soar over the river corridor. Late spring and early fall are the best times to see the many reptiles and amphibians in the park. Black rat snakes, eastern kingsnakes, midland water snakes, and copperheads are frequently seen. An early morning or early evening stroll along the river can be most rewarding. Even if you don't see an animal, tracks, scat, and other signs of wildlife are abundant along the trails.

Directions: Paces Mill Unit — From I-285, take exit 14 (US Hwy. 41). Travel south 1.5 miles to Unit entrance on the right. Island Ford Unit — From I-285, take exit 19 (GA Hwy. 400). Travel north 5 miles to exit 6 (Northridge Rd.) and turn right. Cross over GA 400 and continue right onto Dunwoody Place. Travel .5 miles, turn right on Roberts Drive, and travel .7 miles to Island Ford Parkway on the right. Entrance is marked.

Management: National Park Service, 770-399-8070

Closest Town: Atlanta, GA

Site Notes: observation platforms, interpretive programs

Additional Information: Trail maps and river maps can be obtained at no cost at the visitor contact stations at Paces Mill and Island Ford. A bird checklist is also available at these sites.

Classic South

In the Classic South travel region, the wildlife watcher will find more of the piedmont cotton fields of 1850 now in second-growth timber and various stages of "old field succession" vegetation. This region includes the upper Savannah River Valley with most of the river existing now in the form of hydropower impoundments. Great opportunities exist for recreation and wildlife viewing. There are also stretches of the natural river and its floodplain, which form the eastern border of the State. The vegetation occurring on the river bluffs in the Coastal Plain south of Augusta tends to be more closely associated with the mountains. Tributary streams to the Savannah from the Georgia side exhibit outstanding examples of hardwood swamps and cypress swamps, which form excellent wildlife habitats. South of Augusta, most of these tributaries are slow-moving blackwater streams, some of them containing very old hardwood trees. These areas were spared the impact of human agriculture because they were too wet to farm and too low to drain.

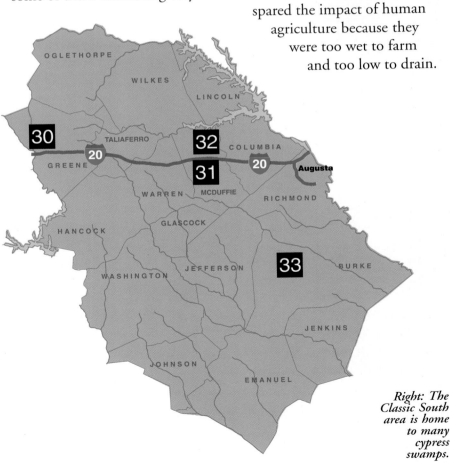

Right: The Classic South area is home to many cypress swamps.

KAREN LAWRENCE

Bald eagles visit the wetlands of Dyar Pasture to search for food.

30 Dyar Pasture M.A.R.S.H. Project

Description: This is a joint waterfowl habitat creation project of the State Wildlife Resources Division and Ducks Unlimited, a non-profit waterfowl conservation organization. The result is a 50-acre wetland complex adjacent to beautiful Lake Oconee. The water level in shallow ponds is lowered during spring and summer to allow waterfowl food plants to grow. These ponds are then flooded during fall and winter to provide resting sites and access to food plants and seeds for waterfowl. Surrounding Dyar Pasture, Lake Oconee and the Oconee National Forest provide many additional wildlife viewing and outdoor recreation opportunities.

Viewing Information: There are year-round opportunities for excellent bird watching at this ever-changing wetland complex. Each season with its changing water level and food availability brings a new mix of species. Spring and summer bring great blue herons, little blue herons and numerous shore birds to feed in the shallow waters. Ospreys and bald eagles that nest on Lake Oconee might be seen feeding here as well. Wood storks may use the area if fish are concentrated in isolated pools during August and September. The ideal conditions for prey species also make ideal conditions for predators, so bobcats, foxes, coyotes, minks, otters, and other predators are seen frequently. The varied habitats surrounding this project are home to many species of songbirds. During fall and winter these flooded ponds attract wood ducks, mallards, blue-winged teals and, occasionally, pintails. The mixed pine-hardwood forests around this area have high populations of white-tailed deer, wild turkeys, gray squirrels and raccoons. An extensive road system throughout the National Forest provides access to many excellent wildlife viewing areas.

Directions: From Madison, travel US Hwy. 278 east. Cross the Apalachee River into Green County and then turn left onto the third paved road. Travel apx. .8 miles into the community of Greshamville and turn right on the first paved road at the Methodist Church. Travel apx. 2.3 miles, crossing Greenbriar Creek, to the entrance. Follow Forest Service Road 1267 through the pasture to the parking area. Gravel foot path from the parking area leads north to the impoundment.

Management: Georgia DNR, Wildlife Resources Division, 770-918-6416; U.S. Forest Service, 706-485-7110

Closest Town: Madison, GA

Additional Information: Spotting scopes or binoculars are very helpful for viewing birds from a distance in the impoundment.

31 McDuffie Public Fishing Area

Description: Thirteen fishing lakes and numerous fish rearing ponds are scattered over 560 acres. Located in the Fall Line sand hills region of the State, this site is predominantly dry uplands of deep, sandy soil supporting remnant stands of longleaf pine and turkey oak. This habitat was once common in Middle and South Georgia, but today much of it has been converted to industrial pine plantations. Numerous wetland areas are found adjacent to the fishing lakes and provide an interesting contrast to the dry uplands.

Viewing Information: McDuffie PFA is a wonderful site for easy viewing of the wildlife once common to these dry longleaf pine habitats. A large population of big black-masked fox squirrels is found here and can be seen feeding on pine seeds

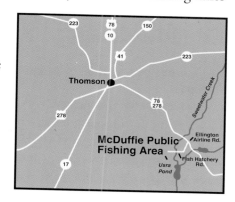

they pick from longleaf pine cones. This is an excellent birding area. Look for yellow-breasted chats, prairie warblers, and orchard orioles. The ponds and wetland areas are home to great blue herons, great egrets, ducks, Canada geese, river otters, beavers, and wild turkeys. Osprey nest in the area and can be seen soaring overhead with red-tailed hawks, red-shouldered hawks, and black and turkey vultures. Listen for quail, owls, and the whippoorwill. Winter brings grebes, coots, mallards, hooded mergan-

The call of the barred owl is one of the most distinctive night-time sounds of forested swamps.

sers, and green-winged teal to feed in the ponds and wetlands. The PFA is open year-round, from sunrise to sunset, seven days a week.

Directions: From Thomson, travel south on GA Hwy. 17. Turn east (left) on US Hwy. 78/278 and travel 5.6 miles. Go right on Ellington Airline Road for 2.8 miles. Turn right on Fish Hatchery Road and go 1 mile.

Management: Georgia DNR, Wildlife Resources Division, 706-595-1684

Closest Town: Thomson, GA

Site Notes: fishing piers, archery range, fishing skills range, interpretive trail, dove field, kids' fishing events

32 Mistletoe State Park

Description: Find here two thousand acres of varied Piedmont habitats and 6 miles of trails situated on beautiful 70,000-acre Clarks Hill Lake. Once worn-out farmlands, this area has regenerated to mixed pine and hardwood forests, beaver swamps, and hardwood creek bottoms. Deeply eroded "canyons" are evidence of past erosive farming practices. Also present are many young forests of loblolly pine, sweetgum, tulip poplar, red maple, and white oak. Creek bottoms offering spring wildflower displays of trillium, striped pipsissewa, bloodroot, Christmas fern, and cinnamon fern are found in the many lake coves surrounding the park. An observation deck overlooks a deep gully and waterfall on Claitt Creek Trail, and a wildlife observation area along Loop Trail offers an excellent opportunity for viewing.

Viewing Information: Large flocks of resident Canada geese are regularly seen in the many coves of Clarks Hill Lake. Mallards, ring-necked ducks, wood ducks, and wading birds might also be seen by the observant visitor. Old fields and the wildlife observation area are excellent sites for viewing wild turkeys, white-tailed deer, red and gray foxes and numerous songbirds. The visitor with a boat or canoe has many opportunities to explore the numerous quiet coves in the park. A large area of the southeastern portion of the park is without trails, receiving little visitation, and is suited for those who want quiet and solitude to hike cross-country.

Directions: From Thomson, travel I-20 to exit 60. Turn north on GA Hwy. 150 (Cobb Ham Rd.) and travel 7.9 miles. Turn left on Mistletoe Road and travel 3 miles to park entrance.

Management: Georgia DNR, Parks and Historic Sites Division, 404-656-2770

Closest Town: Thomson, GA

Site Notes: interpretive programs, cottages, fishing

RICHARD T. BRYANT

One of six venomous snakes found in Georgia, the copperhead is often found in urban areas.

63

33 Di-Lane Plantation Wildlife Management Area

Description: Di-Lane Plantation is an 8,100-acre WMA situated in Georgia's Upper Coastal Plain. About 70 percent of the area is forested, primarily in natural stands of upland hardwoods and pines. The understory varies from dense thickets of palmetto, wax myrtle,

RICHARD T. BRYANT

The bobcat finds ample rodents and other prey in the forest and fields on the plantation.

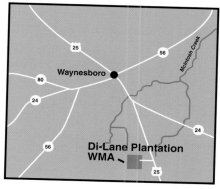

and gallberry to open grassy meadows. The remaining 30 percent is in various stages of old-field succession intermixed with wildlife plantings to enhance habitat. The area has some outstanding wetland habitats that harbor many species of native resident and migratory wildlife. Laurel oaks draped in Spanish moss line the entrance road that passes a pet cemetery established by a previous owner in tribute to his bird dogs.

Viewing Information: In addition to providing habitat for game birds, such as bobwhite quail, mourning doves, and wild turkeys, Di-Lane Plantation is also home to many nongame birds, including bluebirds, sparrows, and warblers. During the late fall and early spring, large numbers of hawks can be observed hunting the open fields. Many wood ducks and a variety of other waterfowl roost throughout the area in winter. Other common winter wetland birds include great blue and green herons and occasionally wood storks. The abundant early successional habitats intermixed with mature forests maintain high populations of prey species, including rabbits, fox squirrels and gray squirrels, white-tailed deer and numerous rodents. Because of the excellent populations of prey, Di-Lane is a good place to observe predators such as gray and red foxes, bobcats and coyotes. Other common mammals include raccoons, opossums, skunks, and beavers. River otters are occasionally observed. Several species of bats commonly occur in the area. A variety of turtles, frogs, salamanders, and snakes occur throughout the area. Three of Georgia's six venomous snakes are found here, including cottonmouths, copperheads, and timber rattlesnakes. The American alligator is a common summer sight.

Directions: From Waynesboro, take 4th Ave./Herndon Rd. south 10 miles and follow signs to the check station.

Management: Georgia DNR, Wildlife Resources Division, 706-595-4222

Closest Town: Waynesboro, GA

Historic Heartland

Both history and wildlife viewing of high quality are found in the geographic heart of the State. The Historic Heartland is characterized by rolling piedmont forests of second-growth pine and hardwood river swamps. The swamps occur in significant acreage along the Ocmulgee and Oconee Rivers after they pour over the Fall Line into the Coastal Plain near Macon and Milledgeville, respectively. These swamps provide some of the most significant wildlife habitat in the State. Many smaller rivers in the area provide opportunities to study both human and natural history. The Towaliga River at the Fall Line, and the Alcovy, Yellow, and South rivers farther north in the area, provide much of the water to continue the seasonal floods below the Fall Line. The Alcovy drainage in Newton and Walton Counties contains river swamps that are remnants of the ancient Coastal Plain. The mature forest habitats of Piedmont National Wildlife Refuge provide an unusual haven for deep forest wildlife. By contrast, most of the area was in agriculture, principally cotton, in the 1850s. By 1900, the eroded cotton fields were reverting to timber species which have been managed and harvested several times since then. This silvicultural practice has contributed to a continuing "old field succession" which promotes wildlife diversity in the area, especially among birds that require open space.

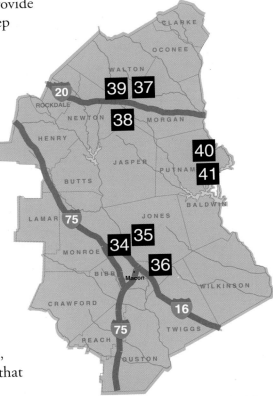

Right: The red-cockaded woodpecker, Georgia's only woodpecker to excavate nest cavities in living pines.

34 Rum Creek M.A.R.S.H. Project

Description: This M.A.R.S.H. (Matching Aid to Restore State Habitat) project is one of 18 similar public-private partnerships across the State sponsored by Ducks Unlimited. It is one of the best locations in the State to see a wide variety of waterfowl. Managed specifically for waterfowl, this 32-acre complex includes a green tree reservoir, winter-flooded row crops, scrub/shrub wetlands, and open water. Thousands of ducks and geese call this refuge home for the winter. The adjacent 6,000-acre Rum Creek Wildlife Management Area and 3,600-acre Lake Juliette offer additional excellent wildlife viewing opportunities.

Viewing Information: In winter months, thousands of migratory birds descend on this waterfowl haven. Mallards, wood ducks, gadwalls, shovelers, ring-necked ducks, green-winged teal and blue-winged teal are regular visitors. Early mornings and late afternoons is when you will see the most waterfowl. Wading birds, marsh and shorebirds such as herons, egrets, woodcocks, snipes, and killdeer are also common. Overhead soar numerous species of hawks and, occasionally, bald eagles. The shallow water and intermittent wetland areas are excellent sites to search for bull frogs, green treefrogs, salamanders, water snakes, and snapping turtles on warm summer days.

Directions: From Forsyth, travel Juliette Road (exit 61 on I-75) east for 3.6 miles to the Rum Creek M.A.R.S.H. Project sign on the left. Proceed to the next gated road on the left. Park at the gate and walk down the road to the dike of the impoundment.

Management: Georgia DNR, Wildlife Resources Division, 912-825-6354

Closest Town: Forsyth, GA

Additional Information: Maps of Rum Creek Wildlife Management Area and a detailed map of the M.A.R.S.H. Project are available from Georgia DNR (912-994-2439).

RICHARD T. BRYANT

Choruses of green treefrogs may be heard calling from spring through late summer.

35 Piedmont National Wildlife Refuge

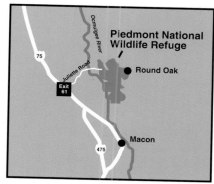

Description: The refuge is 35,000 acres of predominantly loblolly pine on the ridges with hardwoods found along creek bottoms and in scattered upland coves. Clear streams and beaver ponds provide ideal wetland habitat for migrating waterfowl. Old-growth pine forests that support a colony of endangered red-cockaded woodpeckers can be found. The population on the refuge is the only known population in the Piedmont region of Georgia. The rich diversity of habitats provides a haven for nearly 200 species of birds and many mammals.

Viewing Information: Red-cockaded woodpeckers can be seen in the spring from mid-April to mid-June during the nesting season. This is also a great time to watch for migrating songbirds, especially spring warblers. Spring migration begins in March and peaks in April through early May, and fall migration peaks in September and October. A bird checklist for the refuge is available at the visitors center. Late November through January are the best months to see waterfowl. A six-mile auto drive and three foot trails are open during daylight hours year-round. Approximately 50 miles of gravel roads are also open for public travel, except during limited fall white-tailed deer hunts. Caution should be used on these roads during wet weather. Resident songbirds, turkeys, white-tailed deer, fox squirrels, gray squirrels, and much of the other wildlife found on the refuge can be seen from these roads and trails. The refuge visitors center is open Monday through Friday 8 a.m. to 4:30 p.m., and weekends 9 a.m. to 5 p.m., except on federal holidays. Refuge staff are available to assist and orient visitors in finding the best viewing areas and times. Those interested in group programs and tours involving staff should make reservations at least two weeks in advance.

Directions: From Atlanta, take I-75 south to exit 61. Travel east on Juliette Road 18 miles. Entrance is marked.

Management: U.S. Fish and Wildlife Service, 912-986-5441

Closest Town: Round Oak, GA

Site Notes: observation platforms, tours, interpretive programs, six-mile auto driving tour, hunting, fishing

Additional Information: Georgia's Jarrell Plantation State Historic Site adjoins the refuge. A good day-trip can be made to the refuge and Jarrell Plantation.

KAREN LAWRENCE

Look for the gulf fritillary around the passion flower, the host plant for the fritillary caterpillar.

36 Ocmulgee National Monument

Description: An archaeological and natural history treasure preserved to showcase and interpret 10,000 years of human habitation in the area, Ocmulgee National Monument is uniquely located on the Fall Line sand hills separating the once ocean-covered Coastal Plain from the hilly Piedmont region. This site includes mowed fields, mixed pine-hardwood forest, broad river flood plain and beaver swamps. Here is the beginning of the magnificent Ocmulgee River flood plain which is up to 5 miles wide and extends downriver to its confluence with the Oconee River, forming the great Altamaha. Six miles of trails provide easy access to the wide variety of habitats of the area.

Viewing Information: This site is well-known for its great birding. The northernmost extent of Coastal Plain river flood plain habitat is found here. Birds generally found much farther south may be seen in the area during summer. These include the prothonotary warbler, parula warbler, Swainson's warbler, yellow-crowned night herons, and great egret. Bald eagles, swallow-tailed kites, or Mississippi kites might be seen soaring high over this broad floodplain, searching these remote wetlands for food. White-tailed deer, foxes, bobcats, coyotes, and rabbits are numerous along the trails crisscrossing the upland portion of this National Monument. Several short trails highlight bottomland habitats where beavers, river otters, raccoons, and muskrats can be seen, along with many species of ducks and wading birds.

Directions: From Macon, take I-16 to exit 4 (Coliseum Drive). Go east on US Hwy. 80 apx. 1 mile to the park entrance on the right.

Management: National Park Service, 912-752-8257

Closest Town: Macon, GA

Additional Information: The visitors center houses a significant regional archaeological museum.

37 Hard Labor Creek State Park

Description: A mosaic of upland pine and hardwood forest, steep-walled creek bottoms, granite outcrops, old fields, broad floodplain forest, and man-made lakes make this 5,800-acre park one of the best wildlife viewing sites in North Georgia. A network of 24 miles of trails provides plenty of opportunity to view wildlife in quiet solitude. Floodplain forests consist of river birch, sycamore, green ash, sweetgum, water oak and willow oak. Upland forests include southern red oak, red maple, sweetgum, hickory, sourwood, loblolly pine, and flowering dogwood. This very hilly portion of the Piedmont is particularly breathtaking when the leaves change color in fall.

Viewing Information: Wildlife is abundant throughout the park. The diversity of habitats supports a wide range of species. Songbirds, white-tailed deer and wild turkeys are abundant in the upland forests. Beaver ponds, streams, and man-made ponds provide the best viewing opportunities. At these sites look for river otters, beavers, raccoons, muskrats, red-winged blackbirds, yellow-rumped warblers, and red-billed woodpeckers. Listen for the pileated woodpecker and barred owl. Reptiles and amphibians of the wet areas include bullfrogs, green frogs, box turtles, brown water snakes, and two-lined salamanders. Easy access to the two lakes on the park and the presence of numerous ducks and geese make these spots common stops for wildlife viewers.

Directions: From Atlanta, travel east 50 miles on I-20 to exit 49. Follow signs to park.

Management: Georgia DNR, Parks and Historic Sites Division, 706-557-3001 (Park Office)

Closest Town: Rutledge, GA

Site Notes: 18-hole golf course, cottages, group shelters, group camps, boat and canoe rental, fishing

38 Charlie Elliott Wildlife Center

Description: Charlie Elliott Wildlife Center (CEWC) is located in the Georgia Piedmont and encompasses 6,500 acres. A wide variety of habitat types includes a rock outcrop, old fields, mixed pine/hardwoods, pine stands, and bottomland hardwoods. Approximately half the area is in old field and pasture; however, the pasture is being converted to hardwoods. A large portion of the area is also in pine and hardwoods. The site contains 29 ponds totaling over 300 acres of water. Beaver swamps are found throughout the area on various streams.

Viewing Information: Due to the various habitat types found on CEWC, a wide variety

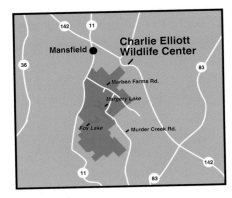

Twenty-nine ponds at the wildlife center offer numerous quiet spots for fishing.

of wildlife, especially birds, can be observed. Red-tailed hawks are seen year-round; marsh hawks may be seen hunting the fields beginning in October and throughout the winter months. Several active barn owl nests are present at the site. Ducks can be observed on any of the 29 ponds throughout the year but especially during the winter months; several species of herons may also be seen along the shores of the ponds. Warblers, sparrows, and woodpeckers are seen throughout the year. Mammals include white-tailed deer, raccoons, skunks, bobcats, fox squirrels, chipmunks and other common small mammals. Beavers and river otters may also be seen in and around the ponds.

Directions: From Mansfield, travel apx. 3 miles south on GA Hwy. 11 and turn left at the Charlie Elliott Wildlife Center sign. The office is 1 mile on the right. Maps may be obtained at the public information boards or at the office.

Management: Georgia DNR, Wildlife Resources Division, 770-784-3059

Closest Town: Mansfield, GA

Site Notes: observation platforms, interpretive programs

Additional Information: Insect and tick repellent are highly recommended. Seed ticks are very common during the summer months.

KAREN LAWRENCE

Opossums, the only marsupial found in North America, have adapted well to living near people.

39 Wildlife Resources Division Headquarters

Description: Less than a one-hour drive from downtown Atlanta, the Wildlife Resources Division headquarters offers wildlife enthusiasts a wide array of wildlife viewing opportunities. The area boasts a one-mile-long environmental education trail that features numbered stations with information on a variety of wildlife-related topics, including birds of the forest, frog ponds, and wetlands. The loop trail is self-guided and a free brochure is available at the office or in the kiosk at the trailhead. This brochure includes a map and additional interpretive information for people walking the trail. This site also features a wildlife nest box exhibit, demonstrating nest boxes suitable for many species of Georgia's backyard wildlife. Adjacent to the office complex is the Division's Walton County Fish Hatchery. The hatchery facility supplies game fish for stocking in Georgia's lakes and ponds. The hatchery is an excellent place to watch for a variety of wading birds and songbirds, as well as other wildlife.

Viewing Information: White-tailed deer are abundant in the upland forests at the site. Wild turkeys are also present, but catching a glimpse of them is a rare occurrence. Two small streams and several abandoned man-made hatchery ponds provide outstanding viewing opportunities. At these sites look for great blue herons, green herons, egrets, Canada geese, otters, raccoons, muskrats, red-winged blackbirds, and yellow-rumped warblers. Reptiles and amphibians of the wet area include bullfrogs, green frogs, box turtles, brown water snakes and two-lined salamanders. A variety of woodpeckers can be easily observed from the trail, including the pileated, red-headed, red-bellied, hairy and downy woodpeckers. Listen for red-tailed hawks during the day and great horned owls very early in the morning. Many songbirds and butterflies can be seen along the trail and in the outstanding gardens of native plants surrounding the headquarters building. These native gardens contain a number of rare plant species and an excellent exhibit of carnivorous pitcherplants. Easy access to the headquarters site makes it a popular stop for wildlife viewers. This is one of the most attractive wildlife agency offices in the nation.

Directions: From Atlanta, travel Interstate 20 east apx. 40 miles to exit 48 (US Hwy. 278). Turn left (north) and travel 1.7 miles to the headquarters sign on the right. Walton County Fish Hatchery is located across the road.

Management: Georgia DNR, Wildlife Resources Division, 770-918-6400

Closest Town: Social Circle, GA

40 Oconee Waterfowl Area and Wildlife Education Trail

Description: Located on the 4,100-acre Oconee Wildlife Management Area and bordering the 19,000-acre Lake Oconee, this is an area of gently rolling hills of mixed pine-hardwood forests laced with numerous small streams. Two (of many) highlights of this area are the waterfowl area and the wildlife education trail. The waterfowl area is a series of managed impoundments just downstream from the dam. Water levels are managed and food plots planted to improve habitat for waterfowl. The wildlife education trail is an excellent natural history interpretive trail. In addition to passing through the waterfowl area, this two-mile trail crosses unique granite outcrops, beaver swamps, old fields, upland forests, and an abandoned rock quarry. Interpretive signs and a teaching guide make this a superb educational facility.

Viewing Information: The waterfowl area offers excellent wildlife viewing from both the ground and an observation deck at the site. Mallards, ring-necked ducks, and teal are numerous during fall and winter. Lucky visitors might spot the rare sandhill crane, which is becoming a regular visitor during migration, or a pair of bald eagles which nest nearby every year. Early morning or late afternoon is the best time to visit the impoundments. Along the wildlife education trail, look for wildlife signs such as beaver tracks and cuttings, white-tailed deer scrapes and rubs, turkey scratching, and fox scat. Bird watching is excellent in the spring over the entire trail. Vireos, woodpeckers, warblers, and hawks all make this lakeside refuge home.

Directions: Take GA Hwy. 16 East from Eatonton apx. 13 miles to the Georgia Power road. Turn left to Lawrence Shoals Recreation Area. The trail entrance is about 100 yards on the right.

Management: Georgia DNR, Wildlife Resources Division, 770-918-6416

Closest Town: Eatonton, GA

Additional Information: This site has an elevated observation platform. Educators wanting information about using the trail for their classes should contact Georgia DNR at 770-918-6416.

41 Baldwin State Forest Wildlife Management Area/Public Fishing Area

Description: This is a 2,500-acre tract located on the northern edge of the Coastal Plain. The site offers an opportunity to observe the upper limits of the longleaf pine habitat in the mid-state. The southernmost portion of the site is a very diverse wildlife viewing area, consisting of beaver ponds, wooded swamps, shrub swamps, and longleaf pine uplands. A number of the former beaver ponds and open marsh sites have reverted to shrub swamp heavily vegetated in alder and maple. In some openings, emergent needle rush is predominant; an area of open water remains, as well as a small portion of wooded swamp having black gum as the dominant overstory. A few acres of relict sand dune habitat exist on the extreme southwest corner with characteristic scrub oak overstory and sparse ground cover. The PFA consists of five ponds that encompass 51 acres of water, providing angling for channel catfish, largemouth bass, and bream. Several of the ponds are managed intensively for channel catfish. The layout of the area allows for very good fishing and wildlife viewing at the same time.

Viewing Information: A late summer afternoon is likely to produce several Mississippi kites soaring above the Baldwin PFA ponds. An occasional osprey may be seen fishing over the ponds and waterfowl of several species may stop for a rest during the winter months. Great blue herons, and snowy and common egrets are familiar sights but are most frequent in spring when they are also most handsome in their breeding plumage. Beaver ponds, shrubs, and wooded swamps offer more habitat variety but are generally very thick. Wood ducks, herons, egrets, beavers, raccoons, and cottonmouths may be found here. Late spring and fall migrant songbirds may be found in good numbers and variety. The small stand of longleaf pine offers an increasingly rare opportunity to experience a southern pine forest with its distinct aroma, sights, and sounds. These pines support pine siskins, Carolina wrens, and a wide variety of woodpeckers. The very small area of scrub oak presents the chance to observe another disappearing habitat, with associated wildlife species such as the gopher tortoise and eastern diamondback rattlesnake.

Directions: From Milledgeville travel south on US Hwy. 441. Go apx. 3 miles south of the GA Hwy. 243 intersection to the point where the highway crosses Little Black Creek. Follow signs to entrance of PFA.

Management: Georgia DNR, Wildlife Resources Division, 912-825-6151 (general information), 912-453-4200 (fishing area), 912-825-6354 (management area)

Closest Town: Milledgeville, GA

Additional Information: Milledgeville was the capitol of Georgia during the Civil War. The old governor's mansion, old State Capitol building, historic district featuring many pre-Civil War houses, Georgia College, Lake Sinclair, and other points of interest are located near the viewing site. Motels, restaurants, and shopping opportunities may also be found in Milledgeville.

Presidential Pathways

After leaving Atlanta, the Chattahoochee River travels through this area and then crosses the Fall Line just south of West Point, where it becomes the border with adjoining Alabama. This land is part of the Apalachicola watershed, which includes the Chattahoochee River and the Flint River. The Flint River is a very special place with spectacular natural features like Sprewell Bluff, Dripping Rock, and Yellow Jacket shoals; tributaries like Potato Creek with its spider lilies and Big Lazer Creek; and the many other streams that spill through deep ravines. The ravine forests here contain a rich mix of mountain, coastal plain and piedmont plant and animal species. Pine Mountain, the southernmost mountain in the State, provides a surprising opportunity for scenic vistas otherwise available only in extreme north Georgia. Located on the east end of the mountain, Warm Springs was the favored home of President Franklin Delano Roosevelt, who found relief from his polio pain in these natural waters. The home of President Jimmy Carter is also located on the south end of the area in the town of Plains.

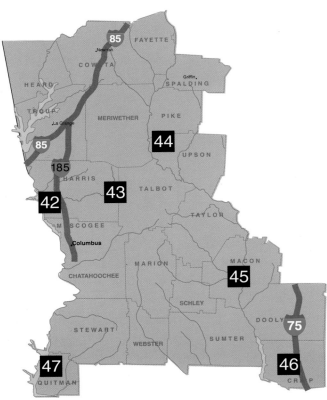

42 Blanton Creek Wildlife Management Area

Description: Blanton Creek WMA is located in Harris County in the Greenville slope district of the southern Piedmont. This 4,500-acre site is characterized by steep, somewhat rocky ridges and ravines along the Chattahoochee River, changing from rolling to gentle hilly terrain. More than half of the habitat on this site is pine and pine-hardwood. Other habitats present include bottomland hardwoods, upland hardwoods, old fields, and wetlands, including a M.A.R.S.H. project. ("M.A.R.S.H." or "Matching Aid for Restoring State Habitat" is a program providing financial assistance sponsored by Ducks Unlimited.)

Viewing Information: Wildlife likely to be observed in any season includes white-tailed deer, wild turkeys, gray squirrels, cottontail rabbits, and many species of songbirds. It is also possible to observe bobwhite quail, raccoons, mourning doves, bald eagles, and various waterfowl along the river and the M.A.R.S.H. project, particularly in the late summer and early fall. Early morning and late evening are excellent times for viewing most of these species, although songbirds and quail may be seen any time. Road conditions vary with the weather but are generally good. The area is closed to wildlife viewing during managed white-tailed deer hunts. Check annual hunting regulations for these dates.

Directions: From West Point, GA, take GA Hwy. 103 south apx. 10 miles to the sign for Blanton Creek WMA. Turn right and proceed to the check station.

Management: Georgia DNR, Wildlife Resources Division, 912-825-6354

Closest Town: West Point, GA

Site Notes: interpretive programs (on request), observation platforms

43 Warm Springs Regional Fisheries Center

Description: This unique site is a combined national fish hatchery, fish health laboratory, and environmental education center. Here you can see how warm-water fish are reared for release to enhance native fish populations. In the education center, learn about the fish and wildlife found in the region. An aquarium displays fish reared at the site or native to the nearby waters.

Viewing Information: Fish reared here, which are vital to the fishery resource of the southeastern U.S., include striped bass, sturgeon and paddlefish. On display in the aquarium are gar, largemouth bass, crappie, catfish, bluegill and redear sunfish as well as a stunning display of thousands of brightly-colored goldfish. On the grounds of the center you might see squirrels, rabbits, white-tailed deer, wild turkeys, turtles, frogs, and many species of songbirds. Hawks are commonly seen perched in the trees around the ponds scanning the fields and wetlands for mice, voles, and frogs.

RICHARD T. BRYANT

An orb-weaver spider, one of the many small creatures that can be spotted by keen observers.

Directions: From Warm Springs, travel GA Hwy. 41 east 1 mile to the Center.

Management: US Fish and Wildlife Service, 706-655-3382

Closest Town: Warm Springs, GA

Additional Information: Aquarium Hours are 7:30 a.m. to 4 p.m. daily; the facility is closed on federal holidays. Tours are available. Little White House is nearby. Special group tours of the hatchery can be arranged in advance with the hatchery manager, Warm Springs National Fish Hatchery, Route 1, Box 515, Warm Springs, GA 31830-9712.

44 Sprewell Bluff Park and Wildlife Management Area

Description: The park is a 200-acre rugged area of steep river bluffs and rock outcrops formed by the Flint River cutting through Oak Mountain on its way to the Gulf of Mexico. It is a unique area of the Piedmont where both mountain and Coastal Plain plants and Piedmont and Coastal Plain animals are common. The plant assemblage, rugged geology, rare species, and scenic beauty of this area give it great educational and scientific value. Surrounding the park are 1,200 acres of public hunting lands that provide a protective buffer for this ecologically fragile site.

Viewing Information: This is a very scenic area any time of the year but is particularly magnificent during fall leaf color. The bluff park is a great place for viewing songbirds, particularly in the spring when this is a regular stop for those in migration. Migratory songbirds that might be seen include the hooded warbler, Arcadian flycatcher, summer tanager, eastern wood-pewee, and red-eyed vireo. White-tailed deer, wild turkeys, gray squirrels and raccoons are numerous in the WMA.

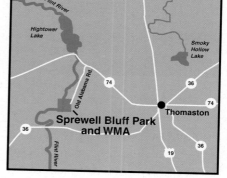

Directions: From Thomaston, GA take GA Hwy. 74 west. Travel 10 miles and look for signs to the Park. Turn left onto Old Alabama Road and travel 6 miles to the WMA check station.

Management: Georgia DNR, Parks and Historic Sites Division, 912-430-4402 (park). The 1,200-acre public hunting area is managed by the Wildlife Resources Division, 912-825-6354.

Closest Town: Thomaston, GA

Site Notes: primitive camping, hunting, fishing

45 Montezuma Bluff Natural Area

Description: A unique and fragile area located in the beautiful and rugged Flint River Valley, this steep, rocky bluff overlooking the river contains beautiful stands of mature hardwood forest. The cool, moist slopes contrasted with hot, dry exposed limestone bluffs harbor a natural community of tremendous diversity. The cool slopes support numerous spring wildflowers, including the very rare and federally protected relict trillium. The dry bluffs are home to sparkleberry, yucca, mountain catchfly, and shortleaf pine.

Viewing Information: This site is primarily known for, and provides protection to, its botanical diversity and plant rarities. The area is also very scenic from the slopes or from the river, which can be accessed by boat ramp. The views from the Flint River are magnif-

icent. Wildlife common to the area include white-tailed deer, wild turkeys, squirrels, and quail. Foxes and raccoons den among the rocky bluffs, and hawks and vultures are common sights soaring above these steep slopes. Seepage areas along the slopes are excellent habitat for

Black vultures are often seen soaring high above the steep bluffs.

many reptiles and amphibians. Look for the southern ringneck snake, gray rat snake, tiger salamander, marbled salamander, and the broadhead skink on the drier slopes.

Directions: From Montezuma, travel north on GA Hwy. 49 apx. 2.2 miles. Turn left (west) and follow the paved county road for less than 1 mile to a boat ramp. The site lies on either side of road.

Management: Georgia DNR, Wildlife Resources Division, 912-430-4254

Closest Town: Montezuma, GA

Site Notes: parking, boat ramp

Additional Information: Picking or digging plants from this or any other public lands in Georgia is strictly prohibited.

46 Cordele Fish Hatchery/Williams Wetlands

Description: This is a 160-acre fish hatchery, with an associated wetland viewing area. Located in the Upper Coastal Plain, these two adjacent facilities contain 27 hatchery ponds that encompass 20 acres of water and a 40-acre wetland area that is partially flooded to benefit waterfowl. The 27 hatchery ponds are intensively managed to produce a variety of species of fish, including channel catfish, hybrid bass, shoal bass, and golden shiners. These ponds range from .2 to 2.5 acres in size. Below the hatchery and along the Gum Creek flood plain, visitors can view a mature bottomland plant community that contains oak, gum, and baldcypress. In this wetland area, visitors can view ecological succession in progress, including a young community of gum, cypress, and willow trees along with cattails, American alligator weed, and duckweed. Pine trees, both loblolly and longleaf, grow in the uplands. There is also a spring on the hatchery grounds that delivers approximately 200 gallons of water per minute every day.

Viewing Information:
The principal function of the hatchery is to culture fish, and the best seasons for viewing these operations are during the spring spawning and fall harvest activities. Visitors can witness brood fish pairing, egg collection and incubation, fry feeding and rearing, and stocking. Heavy summer plankton blooms limit the visibility of fish in ponds, but morning feeding and water quality monitoring are common activities during this time of year. Due to the narrow dikes with sharp turns, access to the hatchery ponds is by foot travel only. Observation of fish harvesting is allowed from a safe distance. Fall offers the best opportunity to view fish harvest techniques. Around the periphery of the hatchery, watchers will see songbirds, woodpeckers, hawks, ospreys, and cormorants. Small mammals such as rabbits, raccoons, and opossums can also be seen. Winter visitors can see a variety of waterfowl and wading birds. Great blue herons, cormorants; snowy, cattle, and common egrets; wood ducks, blue- and green-winged teal, coots, anhingas, and Canada

geese frequent the area. Sightings of red-tailed and red-shouldered hawks are a reasonable expectation. During the summer, wood storks, American alligators, both poisonous and non-poisonous snakes, and amphibians can be seen. The woody growth around the periphery of the wetland attracts non-migratory species of songbirds, sparrows, brown thrashers, and cardinals year-round. Many small mammals such as rabbits, raccoons, opossums, bobcats, and both red and gray foxes are more likely to be seen in the spring. White-tailed deer may also be seen. This facility is open Monday through Friday from 8 a.m. to 4:30 p.m., except for legal state holidays.

Directions: To reach the hatchery and adjacent Williams Wetland areas, travel west from Cordele on US Hwy. 280 apx. .5 miles to Fish Hatchery Road on the right. Go apx. 2 miles on Fish Hatchery Road to hatchery sign on right. Turn right on Williams Lake Road to enter hatchery. Do not turn into hatchery, but proceed farther down Williams Lake Road for 1 mile to dead end at Williams Wetland viewing area.

Management: Georgia DNR, Wildlife Resources Division, 912-276-2362

Closest Town: Cordele, GA

Site Notes: Hatchery: parking, rest rooms. Williams Wetland: parking, rest rooms, picnic facility, a small building that accommodates up to 20 students for classroom instruction.

Additional Information: A slide presentation on hatchery operations is available for group tours with prior arrangements. Call the phone number above to schedule group tours to Williams Wetland.

47 Eufaula National Wildlife Refuge, Bradley Unit

Description: The Bradley Unit of this Refuge is a 700-acre highly manipulated wetland impoundment located on the banks of the Chattahoochee River known as Lake Eufaula. Water is removed by pumping in the spring and summer to allow wildlife food plants to grow and is added to the impoundment in fall and winter to flood these same plants to attract and feed waterfowl. There are some planted fields of corn and sorghum, along with old fields and islands of gum, willow, and wax myrtle.

The unit is surrounded by a levee, and a cross levee separates the unit into two parts. The levees serve as great observation platforms.

Viewing Information: Between late March and early July the rookery is home to or foraging ground for a variety of nesting wading birds. From about March 15 to June 1 the great blue herons and great egrets may be seen sitting on their eggs and delivering food to their young. Look for American anhinga nests also. By late June, the primary species nesting in the rookery are cattle egrets and little blue herons. Hundreds of cattle egrets may be seen at any time during the summer. Sometimes white ibis are observed in the colony, but it is doubtful that they nest there. Look for wood ducks, ring-necked ducks, hooded mergansers, American wigeons, pied-billed grebes, cormorants, American coots, common gallinules, and other water-dependent bird and mammal species in the flooded timber and freshwater marsh. Be observant of the American alligators at this site. There are several 12-foot-long males and several nests along the levees between May and July. A lucky visitor will see sand-hill cranes or wild turkeys feeding in the agriculture fields. Eastern bluebirds and loggerhead shrikes often perch on the power wires. Great-crested flycatchers, eastern phoebes, and marsh and sedge wrens use the dense stands of plume grass and sedges. In the hedge rows and wooded areas, prothonotary, yellow, magnolia and yellow-rumped warblers and common yellowthroats are very active. Look for two silos that house barn owls, rock doves, and bats.

Directions: From Georgetown, GA, go north on GA Hwy. 39 about 9 miles to the Eufaula National Wildlife Refuge, Bradley Unit. Entrance sign on the left. Park there and enter the unit by foot. From the check station, walk right and travel 1 mile along the levee to the heron and egret rookery.

Management: U.S. Fish and Wildlife Service, 334-687-4065

Closest Town: Eufaula, AL

Site Notes: parking, bicycles allowed

Additional Information: There are two locked gates to pass before you enter the unit. Special arrangements must be made to obtain a gate key to enter the unit by vehicle. Contact the refuge office for details. Otherwise, you must enter the unit on foot. Allow 3-4 hours to hike the levees. Take plenty of drinking water and insect repellent.

Plantation Trace

The natural landscape of southwest Georgia is dominated by pine forests, interspersed with specialized habitats such as Carolina bays, lime sinks, hardwood hammocks, and streams with broad floodplains. The original longleaf pine/wiregrass habitat type, characterized by tall, widely dispersed pines amidst a carpet of grass is now rare, but can still be found on some of the stately southern plantations of the area. It is also present on a few sites that are open to the public. This is one of the most fragile habitats in the southern United States. Although maintained by occasional naturally occurring fire, wiregrass is unable to recover from human disturbances to the soil and natural ground cover. The Chattahoochee and Flint Rivers converge here at Lake Seminole to form the Apalachicola as it begins its run to the Gulf of Mexico. Carolina bays, like Grand Bay, support a remarkable array of wildlife. Such wetland habitats, combined with the upland forests of the area, make this corner of Georgia most appealing to wildlife enthusiasts.

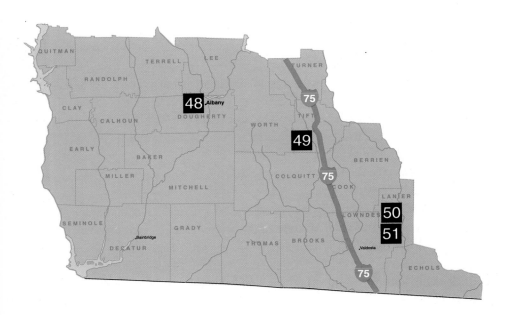

Right: Banks Lake National Wildlife Refuge

48 Albany Nursery Wildlife Management Area Wildlife Trail

Description: Albany Nursery WMA is located in the Upper Coastal Plain in an area of the State known for its large quail plantations. Traditionally an agricultural area, the WMA has a good mixture of fields and forest that appeals to a wide variety of wildlife species. The wildlife trail forms a 2-mile loop through a mature lowland hardwood forest that provides drainage for nearby upland areas. The trail winds under a large hardwood canopy with scattered large pines and follows the edge of a forested wetland that often holds water during the late winter and early spring months. It then circles a stand of mature pines where management using prescribed burning is demonstrated. A number of wildlife management principles are exhibited on the trail.

Viewing Information: White-tailed deer, wild turkeys, bobcats, foxes, raccoons, gray squirrels, wood ducks, and barred owls are some of the more common species that inhabit the area. Various species of hawks can be seen hunting for prey over the fields near the trail. During the spring and fall, many species of songbirds can be observed. Several other species of non-game birds are year-round residents and provide regular opportunities for bird watchers. Viewing of most wildlife species is more productive during the early morning or late afternoon periods, but certain species, like the great blue herons and the common egret, can be observed almost any time of the day. The trail is closed on Wednesdays.

Directions: From Albany, take GA Hwy. 234 (Gillionville Hwy.) west 11 miles. Turn right on Tallahassee Road, and go 1.2 miles to entrance marked by Wildlife Resources Division sign. Parking area and start of trail are just inside entrance.

Management: Georgia DNR, Wildlife Resources Division, 912-430-4254

Closest Town: Albany, GA

Additional Information: Insect repellent is recommended.

49 Paradise Public Fishing Area

Description: Paradise PFA is a unique combination of 71 lakes and ponds totaling 550 acres of water, 568 acres of forested land, and 123 acres of open fields and roads. Habitat types include wetlands, upland pine, planted pine, pine savannas, longleaf pine/wiregrass, and mixed hardwood. The area is intertwined with roads and trails providing visitors passage to much of the area. Slightly rolling hills covered with pines slope down to lake banks and distinct wetland habitats. Lake shorelines, cypress-gum ponds, and branch swamps provide habitats for a variety of wading birds and waterfowl. Clusters of pond cypress and black gum surrounded by water provide an ideal resting spot for wood storks and herons. In contrast, a large longleaf pine/wiregrass community located on the south side of the area provides a perfect habitat for gopher tortoises and a variety of snakes.

Viewing Information: Paradise PFA, managed primarily for public fishing, is also a paradise for those looking for an unforgettable wildlife viewing experience. Numerous species of birds, mammals, and reptiles are found within the boundary. Bald eagles visit the area beginning in October and stay until mid-March. It is common to see them catching shad from Lake Patrick and finishing the freshly-caught meal atop a large longleaf pine. Sometimes pairs can be observed clasping talons and squealing loudly while falling away toward earth, waiting until the last instant to release their clasp. Osprey are frequently seen throughout the year over the lakes hunting for fish or resting while perched atop standing timber in Lake Paradise. Marsh hawks, red-tailed hawks, and red-shouldered hawks can be seen perched on power poles or flying low hunting for food. Wood storks, Canada geese, wood ducks, white ibis, tufted titmice, pied-billed grebes, common loons, pintails, hooded mergansers, green-winged teal, blue-winged teal, and common gallinules are just a few of the birds that can be observed in the area. Migrating birds can be viewed mainly in the fall and winter months.

Mammals include white-tailed deer, bobcats, coyotes, river otters, striped skunks, beavers, gray foxes, gray squirrels, nine-banded arma-dillos, and an abundance of cottontail rabbits. Gopher tortoises are common in and around the longleaf pine/wiregrass plant communi-ties. Tortoises can be found feeding and digging burrows throughout the summer months. Their activity decreases in November, and they are not frequently observed until late Feb. and March. Eastern dia-mondback rattlesnakes are common throughout the upland areas. Timber rattlesnakes, although present, are far less numerous. Many interesting non-venomous snakes such as the eastern kingsnake, east-ern hognose snake, and the gray rat snake are found in abundance along the roadways and in brush piles near open fields. A rare find would be the indigo snake, which has been seen during the summer months on the south side of the area.

Directions: Paradise Public Fishing Area is located 8 miles east of Tifton on the Brookfield-Nashville Road, off US Hwy. 82 near Brookfield, GA. Directions are well-marked on US Hwy 82.

Management: Georgia DNR, Wildlife Resources Division, 912-533-4792

Closest Town: Tifton, GA

Additional Information: Most of the area can be viewed from a vehicle or small boat except for the longleaf pine/wiregrass, and gopher tortoise communities. These areas are accessible only by foot. If you are planning to venture off any of the roads or trails, snake leggings are recommended. Some areas are very delicate and visitors should take care during viewing to minimize disturbance.

50 Banks Lake National Wildlife Refuge

Description: Banks Lake National Wildlife Refuge is 3,500 acres and part of the second largest freshwater ecosystem in the Coastal Plain. It is approximately 12 miles from Grand Bay Wildlife Management Area. The refuge offers 1,000 acres of open water dot-ted with huge cypress trees. The open water is ecologically distinct from the remainder of the 13,000-acre wetland system of which it is a part. It forms the base of a very popular freshwater public fishery including largemouth bass, chain pickerel, bream, and crappie. This open water is maintained by an earthen sill that was constructed in 1825.

The great egret finds an excellent home in extensive wetlands areas like Banks

Viewing Information: Banks Lake provides an excellent opportunity to see winter waterfowl such as widgeon, blue- and green-winged teal, wood ducks, and occasionally, American golden-eyes. The numbers are not vast, but the viewing conditions are good. However, the most spectacular opportunity here is to see osprey and bald eagles, both of which currently nest on the site. The possibility of seeing young fishing over the open water is worth the trip. Good binoculars are a must for this treat. In spring and summer, expect to encounter the full wildlife diversity of the Coastal Plain, as well as some human traffic attracted to the good fishing in Banks Lake.

Directions: From Lakeland, travel west on GA Hwy. 122 for 2-3 miles. Entrance is on the left.

Management: U.S. Fish and Wildlife Service, 912-496-7836 (managed as a satellite refuge of Okefenokee NWR)

Closest Town: Lakeland, GA

Site Notes: accessible fishing pier, concession building

51 Grand Bay Wildlife Management Area

Description: Grand Bay WMA is located in the lower Coastal Plain physiographic province in what is typically known as "flatwoods." It is situated within a 13,000-acre wetlands system, which is the second largest natural blackwater wetland in the Coastal Plain of Georgia. In many ways, the large, shallow, peat-filled wetlands of Grand Bay mimic their big brother, the Okefenokee Swamp. Grand Bay is one of the land features known as "Carolina bays" which, according to one theory, were created by showers of meteors. Plant communities within these bays are a mosaic of wet savannas, shrub

RICHARD T. BRYANT

bogs, cypress-gum ponds, prairie and black gum-cypress swamps, practically indistinguishable from habitats found in the Okefenokee. The diversity of wildlife also compares favorably with that found in the Okefenokee. Uplands surrounding the wetlands provide good examples of mature longleaf-slash pine flatwoods. A small percentage of the area is in mixed live oak-pine and is home to gopher tortoises and indigo snakes. Dudley's Hammock, a rare example of a mature broadleaf-evergreen hammock community, is found in the area.

An immature little blue heron, displaying traces of the gray-blue color it will have as an adult.

Viewing Information: Carolina bays by nature tend to be inaccessible because of their large size (Old Field Bay at Grand Bay WMA is 6,000 acres) and the impenetrable nature of shrub communities surrounding them. A .5-mile boardwalk provides access through a cross section of communities on Grand Bay (a 1,400-acre Carolina bay on the WMA). At the end of the boardwalk is a 54-foot-high observation tower overlooking open prairie and a heron rookery in the bay's center.

In spring, prothonotary warblers arrive and add to the swamp's color with fleeting flashes of gold. The "sweet, sweet, sweet" calls of advertising males echo through black gum and cypress trees. Frequently observed wading birds include cattle and great egrets; great blue, little blue, green and tri-color herons; and white ibis. Anhingas are also common on the marsh. Common moorhens and purple gallinules nest here also. Rarely seen but present are American bitterns, black-crowned and yellow-crowned night herons. A small population of Florida sandhill cranes has been introduced to the area, and individuals can be seen or heard throughout the year. Migratory greater sandhill cranes usually arrive on the marsh in mid-November and remain until mid-January. Several hundred cranes typically feed on the floating mat community in Grand Bay during winter.

Throughout summer, the surface of the prairie is covered by the blooms of fragrant water lilies. A cacophony of sounds can be heard coming from the heron rookery. American alligators of all sizes patrol the surface hunting for prey. Pig frogs and cricket frogs provide a continuous backdrop of sound for the scene. The floating mat community is home to the Florida water rat, a species discovered to inhabit Grand Bay in 1987. Late March and April are the best months to see the turban-shaped grass houses of this aquatic rodent. River otters are commonly observed on the WMA, particularly in late winter. White-tailed deer, raccoons, bobcats, gray foxes, opossums and armadillo are also common. Moon-lit summer nights are an excellent time to enjoy the boardwalk. Pig frogs and cricket frogs continue their rhythm and are joined by barred owls and chuck-will's widows.

Directions: From Valdosta take US Hwy. 221 north apx. 10 miles and turn left on Knight's Academy Road. Go 1.5 miles to the entrance sign on the right. The entrance road leads 1 mile north to a "T". The boardwalk is to your left, the interpretive center and canoe trail entrance to your right.

Management: Georgia DNR, Wildlife Resources Division, 912-423-2988
Closest Town: Valdosta, GA
Site Notes: observation tower, boardwalk, canoe trail
Additional Information: A canoe trail brochure with directions and information on the area's wetlands can be obtained by contacting the Valdosta-Lowndes County Convention and Visitor's Bureau at 1-800-569-8687. Moody Air Force Base is adjacent to Grand Bay.

Magnolia Midlands

Geology is dramatic in this area of Georgia in many of the ways that geology is dramatic in the Ridge and Valley province of the northwest corner of the state. Ancient sand ridges along the northeast banks of blackwater rivers support plant and animal communities adapted to dry, hot conditions containing impressive dramatic species, such as indigo snakes, gopher tortoises, the rare Georgia plume, turkey oak, and longleaf pine. Blackwater rivers, like Ohoopee, Canoochee, Satilla, and Willacoochee, exemplify the image of world-famous south Georgia swamps with their alligators, snakes, and other spectacular wildlife communities. Georgia's "great river," the Altamaha, is formed here by confluence of the Ocmulgee and the Oconee as they run to the sea.

52 Beaverdam Wildlife Management Area (Laurens Tract)

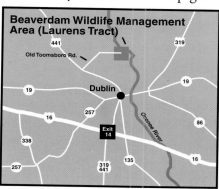

Description: The Beaverdam WMA consists of 12,000 acres in Wilkinson and Laurens counties. The Laurens County tract, which lies at the Fall Line along the northern edge of the Coastal Plain, offers the opportunity to experience one of the best stands of mature bottomland hardwood on the entire Oconee River. This area has been referred to as the Great Oconee Swamp. The swamp occurs at the point below the flow of the river across the Fall Line. The forest overstory is dominated by oak species, including water, willow, cherrybark, swamp chestnut, and overcup. Other prominent canopy trees are beech, sweetgum, sycamore, baldcypress, and tupelo gum. The understory is characterized by switch cane and palmetto. Big Sandy Creek runs along the northern end of the tract. A small oxbow lake called York's Dead River lies toward the southern end of the property.

Viewing Information: Look for wildlife common to forest and edge habitats. White-tailed deer, wild turkeys, gray squirrels, bobcats, and pileated, downy, and hairy woodpeckers. River otters and beavers are common near the water but both are very wary, so stealth is required to get a good look. Also near the water, blue herons, green herons, and kingfishers can be seen. Spring migrating songbirds such as red-eyed vireos, white-eyed vireos, American redstarts, and scarlet tanagers forage in the tree tops 40-70 feet above the ground. The greatest variety are present in April and May, but these birds may be seen throughout the summer. An American alligator is a rare sight. Cottonmouths, canebrake rattlesnakes, non-venomous snakes, and other reptiles are relatively common. Feral pigs and the non-native coyotes are also common.

Directions: Travel north from Dublin on US Hwy. 441 apx. 4.5 miles. Turn right on Old Toomsboro Road and go apx. 5 miles to Evergreen Church. Turn right and go apx. 3 miles and turn right at boat ramp sign. Follow road to Oconee River. Park at the

boat ramp and walk along the road southward by the river.

Management: Georgia DNR, Wildlife Resources Division, 912-825-6354

Closest Town: Dublin, GA

KAREN LAWRENCE

The threatened gopher tortoise makes its burrows in the dry sandhills found in this area.

53 Dodge County Public Fishing Area

Description: Dodge County PFA boasts a 104-acre lake nestled within a 444-acre tract of land southeast of Eastman in Georgia's middle Coastal Plain. The gently rolling terrain surrounding the lake contains mixed pine/hardwood stands, sand ridges with longleaf pine/wiregrass communities, planted pines, and a mature hardwood bottom. Special habitat features include an Altamaha Grit outcrop and a pitcherplant community. Steve Bell Lake contains numerous coves and points, several shallow creek channels, a small island, some standing timber, and submerged structures for attracting fish. The average depth of the lake is ten feet.

Viewing Information: Dodge County PFA offers a wide variety of wildlife viewing. A belted kingfisher may be perched in the standing timber of the lake while a great blue heron silently works along the shoreline, both searching for a meal. White-tailed deer, red foxes, raccoons, fox squirrels, bobwhite quail, and pileated woodpeckers frequent the woodlands surrounding the lake. Southern flying squirrels are plentiful in the area but are seldom seen because of their nocturnal habits. A walk along the nature trail in the spring will reveal a number of songbirds and blooming native plants, including the "insect-eating" hooded pitcherplant (*Sarracenia minor*) and the trumpet pitcherplant (*Sarracenia flava*). The American alligator inhabits the more remote areas of the lake; they are usually not aggressive but deserve your attention and respect. Observe from a distance and stay out of the water when a gator has been seen. On the sand ridge during the warmer months, a gopher tortoise may be observed foraging on native plants. This habitat also holds many non-venomous snakes as well as a few venomous ones such as the eastern diamondback rattlesnake. From late fall through spring the twilight arrival of Canada geese and wood ducks present an exciting scene as they prepare to roost for the night. Osprey and an occasional bald eagle may be seen during the winter soaring above the lake.

Directions: From Eastman take US Hwy. 341 south for 3 miles. Turn left on County Road 49 (dirt road) and cross the railroad tracks. The PFA is located .6 miles off US Hwy. 341.

Management: Georgia DNR, Wildlife Resources Division, 912-374-6765

Closest Town: Eastman, GA

Site Notes: primitive camping, handicap accessible fishing pier, interpretive nature trail, archery range

Additional Information: The Department of Natural Resources has stocked the lake with largemouth bass, bluegill, redear sunfish, and channel catfish. Fishing is permitted, but a fishing license and a WMA stamp is required.

54 Big Hammock Natural Area and Wildlife Management Area

Description: Big Hammock Natural Area and WMA are located along the north bank of the Altamaha River. The WMA consists of 6,177 acres of primarily bottomland hardwoods with many oxbow lakes and sloughs. The Natural Area includes an adjoining 800-acre sand ridge with a variety of habitat types, ranging from a cypress/gum forest to a turkey oak/longleaf pine forest. The Natural Area is registered as a National Natural Landmark by the National Park Service because of its rare plants, animals, and unique qualities, including a large colony of the Georgia plume (*Elliottia racemosa*).

Viewing Information: Many wildlife species can be seen on the WMA and Natural Area. Songbird viewing is especially good in May and June when a variety is present in the areas. Late May and June is also the best time to view the showy white flowers of Georgia plume. One wading bird rookery containing white ibis, common egret, anhingas, and great blue herons exists on the WMA. Sightings of wood storks, Mississippi kites, swallow-tailed kites, and osprey are common. Sand hill reptiles such as the gopher tortoise, diamondback rattlesnake, and eastern indigo snake occur on the Natural Area. American alligators and various water snakes may be seen in many of the oxbow lakes on the WMA. Mammals that a visitor may encounter include white-tailed deer, raccoons, river otters, bobcats, feral hogs, and small mammals such as rabbits, gray and fox squirrels. The presence of a variety of small rodents is evidenced by their bones and hair in owl pellets, which can be found around the bases of cavity trees.

Road access may be limited at times on the WMA due to excessive rain or if the Altamaha River is at or above flood stage. A 1.3-mile hiking trail is located on the Natural Area and no vehicles are allowed in the Natural Area.

Directions: From Jesup, take GA Hwy. 169 north, apx. 24 miles. The WMA entrance will be just north of the Altamaha River on the right.

Management: Georgia DNR, Wildlife Resources Division, 912-423-2988

Closest Town: Glennville, GA

Site Notes: shooting range

55 Evans County Public Fishing Area

Description: Located in the gently rolling hills of the Claxton Terrace, this 372-acre public fishing area has a diversity of habitats. The 84- and 30-acre fishing lakes lie along a blackwater creek that flows through the area. Forested wetlands composed of maples, bay, gum, oak, and pines are found close to these lakes. A wet meadow of sedges, wax myrtle, bulrushes, and grasses is located alongside the large lake. Upland areas are generally in mixed pine and hardwoods, longleaf pine with wiregrass, pines or hardwoods. Several old field areas with stands of Bermuda grass, beard grass, blackberry, oaks, gum, persimmons, and pine are found in the area. The lakes offer good fishing, scenic views and abundant wildlife viewing.

Viewing Information: Wading birds that feed in the lakes and creeks include great blue and little blue herons; great American, snowy, and cattle egrets; and least bitterns. Other wetland birds common to this area are king rails and American coots. Ospreys and an occasional bald eagle come to the area in the spring and fall to feed on fish which they catch near the surface of the lake. Look for anhingas with out-stretched wings, sunning themselves on logs and tree stumps. In the upland fields, listen for bobwhite quail, mourning doves, and other songbirds. Coyotes, otters, raccoons, bobcats, and beavers also are found on this very diverse area. The American alligator may be seen anywhere on this area.

Directions: From Claxton, travel US Hwy. 280 east 8.5 miles. Turn right and follow the signs.

Management: Georgia DNR, Wildlife Resources Division, 912-685-6424

Closest Town: Claxton, GA

Additional Information: The area is open March 1 through October 31 from sunrise to sunset. For specific regulations in the area please check the State Fishing Regulations. Tours are available.

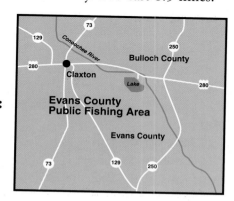

56 General Coffee State Park

Description: Located in the lower Coastal Plain, this site exhibits habitat ranging from sand ridges to gum and cypress river swamps. Containing 1,510 acres, it is the tenth largest state park in land mass. Water features include a number of small lakes through which the Seventeen Mile River winds. The park occupies some of the highest ground in the area, and it is not unusual to find natural rock outcrops, locally called "soap stone outcrops". Approximately 400 acres of prime gopher tortoise and indigo snake habitat have been identified and are actively managed to protect these species and the wildlife community of which they are a part. The Seventeen Mile River swamp boardwalk offers many opportunities to witness endangered and protected plants in their habitats located along the nature trail. The site is well-interpreted with signs, but tours are conducted on request.

Viewing Information: The park is a welcome home to beavers, bobcats, white-tailed deer, black bears, hawks, owls, a variety of songbirds, bald eagles, foxes, herons, kingfishers, gopher tortoises, and indigo snakes. Visitors can actually walk among the burrows of the gopher tortoise and witness these amazing and docile creatures firsthand during warm weather, usually April through early November; they hibernate during the cooler months. Visitors can get up-close and personal with birds of prey at the Christopher L. Morris Raptor Rehabilitation and Education Center located on the park. Some birds must stay here in captivity because their injuries prevent them from surviving in the wild. Others are released when they have recovered.

Directions: From Douglas, travel east 6 miles on GA Hwy. 32 to the park entrance.

Management: Georgia DNR, Parks and Historic Sites Division, 912-384-7082 (Park Office)

Closest Town: Douglas, GA

Site Notes: observation platforms, tours, interpretive programs, pioneer village, archery range, cottages, group shelter.

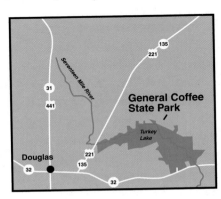

Right: Alligator snapping turtle.

Colonial Coast

The coast of Georgia is rich in colonial history related to the founding and early development of our country. It can also be considered a "gold coast" because it is a dynamic area of growth for people and business. At the same time, this coast represents a tremendous success story in the protection of the natural environment. From the great Okefenokee Swamp, to the mythical barrier islands and their broad beaches, to the mighty Altamaha, Ogeechee, and Savannah Rivers, to the expansive salt marshes, the natural features of the coast of Georgia are afforded more protection than any other part of the state. It is also filled with spectacular opportunities to observe and interact with the natural environment. The Georgia coast is home to a significant industry established to promote and provide recreational opportunities to visit, observe, and commune with the wild places and the wildlife in this most pristine portion of the Georgia natural areas.

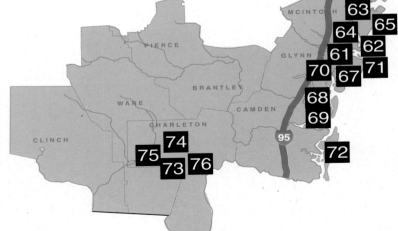

Right: Peaceful beauty is common on the banks of the Altamaha River.

57 Savannah National Wildlife Refuge

Description: Savannah National Wildlife Refuge's 26,295 acres include freshwater marshes, tidal rivers and creeks, bottomland hardwoods, and old rice fields of plantations dating back to the mid- and late-1700s. Many of the dikes enclosing these pools were originally built by slaves and itinerant Irishmen. All dikes are open to foot travel during daylight hours unless otherwise posted and provide excellent wildlife observation points. The Laurel Hill Wildlife Drive meanders along 4 miles of the earthen dikes through managed freshwater pools and hardwood hammocks. About half the refuge is river bottomland composed mainly of cypress, gum, and maple species.

The marshes of the Savannah River support abundant birdlife and offer spectacular sunset views.

Although access to this area is primarily by boat, one dike, the Tupelo Swamp Trail, is located adjacent to the northernmost impoundment and affords visitors hiking opportunities within the bottomland habitat.

Viewing Information: During the winter months, thousands of ducks fill the impoundments, including the rarely-seen cinnamon teal, Eurasian wigeon, and fulvous whistling ducks. More frequently, birders have found tundra swans, greater white-fronted geese, and Canada geese. Other wintering birds include the peregrine falcon, northern harrier, short-eared owl, Virginia rail, common snipe, American woodcock, and a host of song and garden birds, including the American robin, hermit thrush, fox sparrow, and winter wren. Twenty-one species of warblers, including Swainson's, Cape May, worm-eating, blackpoll, black-throated blue, and magnolia, have been seen in spring and autumn migrations. The hardwood hammocks serve to concentrate the songbirds, much to the convenience of the birder. The summer months offer the refuge visitor sightings of purple gallinules and wood ducks, often in the company of their downy offspring, and flocks of white ibis and glossy ibis feeding together.

American alligators are frequently seen on sunny winter days when these reptiles bask along the banks of the canals. The dikes may be temporarily closed to the public (November 1 - March 14) for management purposes. Closed areas are posted accordingly.

American alligators bask along the banks of the canals on sunny winter days.

Directions: From Savannah, travel US Hwy. 17 north across the Talmadge Bridge. Turn left on SC Hwy. 170 south and look for the entrance to the wildlife drive on the left.

Management: U.S. Fish and Wildlife Service, Savannah Coastal Refuges, 912-652-4415

Closest Town: Savannah, GA

Site Notes: observation platforms, wildlife drive.

Additional Information: For refuge maps, bird checklist, or brochure, contact the Savannah Coastal Refuges office: Parkway Business Center, Suite 10, 1000 Business Center Drive, Savannah, GA 31405.

58 Wassaw National Wildlife Refuge

Description: The 10,070 acres that comprise Wassaw National Wildlife Refuge include a single barrier island (Wassaw) and two smaller interior islands. Over three quarters of the refuge is comprised of salt marshes, and nearly one quarter can be categorized as beach, dune, and forest communities. Roads and administrative land account for approximately one percent of the total acreage. Wassaw Island, the largest land mass on the refuge, is one of a chain of barrier islands along the Georgia coast known collectively as the "Golden

RICHARD T. BRYANT

Female loggerhead sea turtles come ashore to lay their eggs from late May to mid-August.

Isles." Wassaw Island is 5.5 miles long, from .5 to 1 mile wide, with 7 miles of ocean beach. It has a prominent central dune ridge running the length of its north to east axis and reaching elevations of nearly 45 feet above sea level. A series of lower dune ridges parallels the main ridge. Numerous depressions and ponds lie between these ridges. Of all the Golden Isles, Wassaw has suffered the least disturbance by man. From the bare sand beach to the old-growth stands of live oak and mixed pine/hardwood climax forest of the central and back dunes, a succession of vegetative habitats provide for an abundance of wildlife species.

Viewing Information: Wassaw is a primary rest stop for neo-tropical migratory birds such as warblers, vireos, and thrushes during spring and autumn migrations. During these migration periods, thousands of shorebirds, such as red knots and several sandpiper species, also utilize the beach habitat for feeding and resting. In fact, the beach is productive for bird watching at virtually any time of the year, and notable sightings have been made during every month. Most exciting are observations of endangered piping plovers, peregrine falcons, and bald eagles (usually in winter), and an occasional reddish egret, roseate spoonbill, or parasitic jaeger (primarily in summer). In summer, tell-tale tracks on the seven-mile-long beach attest to nocturnal visits by the federally threatened loggerhead sea turtles which come ashore for egg-laying then return secretively to the sea. The U.S. Fish and Wildlife Service, in cooperation with the Savannah Science Museum, monitors the nesting activities of the giant loggerheads. Under the supervision of qualified museum personnel, the public is permitted to assist in this ongoing research project. Selected participants must pay a fee covering transportation and lodging expenses. The refuge is open to the public daily during daylight hours. A network of roads and trails throughout the maritime forest appeals to hikers.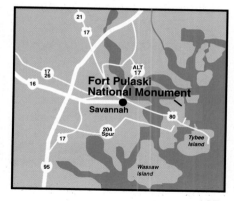

Directions: The refuge is accessible only by boat. Several local marinas in the Savannah area (at Skidaway Island and Isle of Hope), and the public boat ramp adjacent to the Skidaway Island bridge can serve as launching sites for trips to Wassaw.

Management: U.S. Fish and Wildlife Service, Savannah Coastal Refuges, 912-652-4415

Closest Town: Savannah, GA

Additional Information: Visitors planning trips to the island in October and November should contact the refuge office in Savannah and obtain the dates for hunts during which the refuge is closed. Refuge maps, bird checklists, and general informational brochures can also be obtained from the Savannah Coastal Refuges office: Parkway Business Center, Suite 10, 1000 Business Center Drive, Savannah, GA 31405. Boat dock may be used for loading and unloading purposes only.

59 Fort Pulaski National Monument

Description: Named for a celebrated soldier in the American Revolution, this old fort provides an imposing view of 5,200 acres of coastal salt marsh and 300 acres of upland habitat located in the mouth of the giant Savannah River. Moving from the river's edge upland you encounter bands of cordgrass, salt grass, and needle rush, the dominant plant species of this area. Virtually all of the plants are subjected to twice-daily tidal flooding. The small upland area is associated with the grounds of the old fort and consists of maintained lawns and maritime forest. Live oaks, laurel oaks, yaupon holly, and saw palmetto dominate these maritime forests.

Viewing Information: The broad expanses of easily accessible salt marsh make this an excellent site for viewing shorebirds, wading birds, and soaring birds. Herons, egrets, gulls, sandpipers, and plovers are numerous throughout the National Monument area. Wood storks are occasionally seen feeding in small drying ponds in the area. The small isolated patches of maritime forest offer refuge to many migratory songbirds in spring and fall. Numerous species of warblers, swallows, and large flocks of cedar waxwings are common in the spring.

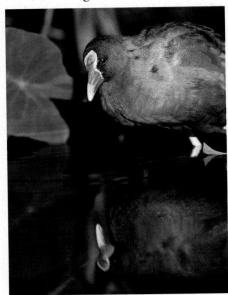

Look for the purple gallinule stalking its prey among the lily pads in fresh water areas.

Forest mammals are surprisingly numerous and include white-tailed deer, bobcats, gray foxes, raccoons, opossums and marsh rabbits. Although a wide variety of reptiles make their homes on monument grounds, they are rarely observed. The secretive eastern diamondback rattlesnake is seen on occasion. The American alligator is sometimes observed in the warmer months, particularly during dry periods, when it may seek the fresh water of the fort's moat. The Atlantic bottle-nosed dolphin is commonly sighted in the Savannah River nearby. An old railroad, nature trail, and constructed dikes make foot travel easy around this area and create opportunities for wildlife watching in solitude. Interpretive programs are available.

Directions: From Savannah, travel 15 miles east on US Hwy. 80 and follow the signs.

Management: National Park Service, 912-786-5787 (Visitors Center)

Closest Town: Tybee Island, GA

60 Harris Neck National Wildlife Refuge

Description: The refuge consists of 2,765 acres of salt-water marsh, grassland, freshwater ponds and mixed deciduous woodlands. The great variety of habitat results in an equally great variety of wildlife. From the Spanish moss-festooned live oak stands to the grasslands, the quiet, observant visitor can be rewarded with ample viewing opportunities. All refuge roads and concrete runways are remnants from the Harris Neck Army Airfield, deactivated in 1944. A 4-mile public access route guides visitors through the refuge. Freshwater ponds and dikes support wading bird rookeries and represent an excellent example of wetland management. Vistas along the wildlife drive offer excellent views of the salt marsh, meandering waterways and upland hammocks. On the east side of the refuge from a high

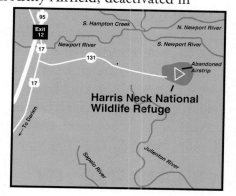

oyster shell bluff overlooking Barbour River, miles of pristine saltmarsh and a few of the island gems that make up Georgia's unique coastal shoreline can be seen.

Viewing Information: The ponds and flooded timber lands located south of the airfield have for many years supported active rookeries for tricolored, green-backed and little blue herons; anhingas; wood storks; and white ibis. (Observe the "closed area" signs posted seasonally when these wading birds are nesting.) Smaller rookeries are located next to the pools between the runways. In spring and summer, wood ducks, purple gallinules, and common moorhens use these ponds. Throughout the colder months many species of dabbling ducks can be found in the refuge ponds. Various species of songbirds are attracted to the woodlands during all seasons. During migration, warblers, vireos, thrushes, and sparrows are abundant. Pileated woodpeckers are seen and heard regularly in the woods, while the wary watcher may observe flocks of wild turkeys feasting on fallen acorns or dusting themselves on sandy roads. Shorebirds can often be seen in the open areas and tidal flats bordering the South Newport and

Barbour Rivers. A variety of raptors, including northern harriers, American kestrels, and, occasionally, a bald eagle or peregrine falcon can be seen in open areas hunting over the refuge grasslands, while ospreys' cries are heard along the marsh edges and over the ponds. Other wildlife sightings include armadillos, opossums, rabbits, feral hogs, raccoons, and white-tailed deer.

Directions: Take exit 12 off I-95 and travel south on US Hwy. 17 for apx. 1 mile. Turn east on GA Hwy. 131 and travel 7 miles to the main entrance gate. To reach the Barbour River Landing, continue on GA Hwy. 131 and follow signs to the landing.

Management: U.S. Fish and Wildlife Service, Savannah Coastal Refuges, 912-652-4415 (Visitors Center)

Closest Town: Darien, GA

Additional Information: Harris Neck National Wildlife Refuge is open to the public daily during daylight hours. Refuge maps, general information brochures, and bird checklists can be obtained from the Savannah Coastal Refuges office: Parkway Business Center, Suite 10, 1000 Business Center Drive, Savannah, GA 31405.

61 Altamaha Waterfowl Management Area

Description: A WMA located in the broad river flood plain of the mighty Altamaha River, this wilderness refuge for wildlife stretches almost 17 miles along the largest undammed river in Georgia. Much of the area is remote and accessible only by boat. Habitats include old diked rice fields, pine savannas, tidal creeks, hardwood floodplain forests, and old-growth stands of baldcypress. Champney and Butler Islands are readily accessible to the visitor without a boat and offer excellent opportunities for seeing songbirds during spring and fall migrations and tremendous numbers of waterfowl during the winter. There are also interesting historic sites here and in nearby Darien.

Viewing Information: For numbers and diversity, this is one of the best areas in the State for observing waterfowl. Old rice fields now serve as managed waterfowl impoundments. Champney Island contains a 34-acre MARSH project, built in 1989 and sponsored by Ducks Unlimited. Great numbers of waterfowl con-

Early morning visitors to the Altamaha WMA are rewarded with colorful sunrises and excellent bird-watching opportunities.

centrate here during the winter. A nature trail and elevated viewing platform are wonderful observation points. In addition to over a dozen species of waterfowl that visit these islands, common sights include the great egret, snowy egret, American bittern, least bittern, and, in the spring, black-necked stilt. Fall migrating songbirds include the common yellowthroat, indigo bunting, and swamp sparrow. Overhead you might see swallow-tailed kites, Mississippi kites or bald eagles. This is a tremendous area for bird watching in a coastal river flood plain habitat.

Directions: From Darien, travel 3 miles south on US Hwy. 17. Turn right on dirt access road across the US Hwy. 17 from the Champney River Boat Landing. The observation tower is .25 mile on the left.

Management: Georgia DNR, Wildlife Resources Division, 912-262-3173

Closest Town: Darien, GA

Additional Information: Area Manager, David Edwards 912-437-6908

62 Fort King George Historic Site

Description: This historic site offers a panoramic view of the famous Georgia spartina marshes, the Altamaha River delta, and distant barrier islands from the fort's restored blockhouse, which stands 40 feet above the ground. The site's short nature trail winds through brackish marsh and maritime forests composed of pine, live oak, red-cedar, and baldcypress mixed with shrubs such as wax myrtle, yaupon holly, and groundsel. Other habitats at the site include tidewater creek and bluff (Black Creek) and holding ponds (18th century man-made tidal sawmill ponds) each of which supports a wide variety of coastal wildlife. Adjoining the fort is one of the oldest British military cemeteries in the southeast. The cemetery contains 65 graves, including 17 marked as the final resting places of British soldiers serving at Fort King George before 1732. Fort King George has been placed on the National Register of Historic Places.

Viewing Information: Today the site abounds in wildlife, in cluding American alligators, snakes, and marsh-loving birds. This site offers very easy access and is a great place to begin the study of birds because the variety is large and the birds are not easily disturbed from their routine. Painted buntings, prothonotary warblers, and the un common Swainson's warbler may be seen in summer. The black-throated blue warbler and the yellow-throated warbler are more likely seen in the winter. Take a careful look at the black vultures soaring overhead. Occasionally one of them will be a white-headed bald eagle soaring with its cousins.

Directions: From I-95, take exit 10 (Darien), turn east on GA Hwy. 251 and go 1 mile to US Hwy. 17. Follow signs. The site is 3 miles off I-95 and is easily accessible.

Management: Georgia DNR, Parks and Historic Sites Division, 912-437-4770 or 912-437-4569

Closest Town: Darien, GA

Site Notes: parking, observation platforms, interpretive programs, museum, audio-visual room

Additional Information: Site is closed before 9 a.m. and after 5 p.m.

63 Blackbeard Island National Wildlife Refuge

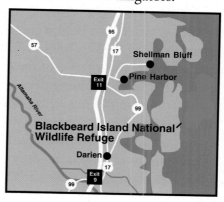

Description: Blackbeard Island is a true barrier island, separated from neighboring Sapelo Island by Blackbeard Creek and an expanse of salt marsh. Geologically, the island is made up of a series of parallel dunes, each of which was once the Atlantic shoreline of a younger island. The 5,618-acre refuge includes a 3,000-acre National Wilderness composed of salt marsh and pine forest on the south end of the island. The north end of Blackbeard is thickly vegetated with palmettos beneath a canopy of live oaks and other hardwoods. Two freshwater impoundments on the north end concentrate ducks in the winter months and wading birds, including the federally endangered wood stork, in the summer. These ponds are populated year-round by great numbers of American alligators.

Viewing Information: Blackbeard Island is open to the public daily during daylight hours. Most visitation occurs along the island's 7 miles of beach. The beach is always alluring, having a wide variety of beach and marine wildlife throughout the year. During winter months, bald eagles and peregrine falcons are often seen from the beach. In the summer, flocks of black skimmers, terns, and brown pelicans congregate along the beach front. A network of roads and trails throughout the interior of the island provides hikers with scenic paths ideal for nature study. Warblers and other songbirds abound in the woodlands. The colorful painted bunting is a regularly-seen summer resident.

Directions: Blackbeard Island NWR is accessible only by boat. Arrangements for trips to the refuge can be made in the town of Shellman's Bluff. From Savannah, travel south on US Hwy. 17 for apx. 51 miles to Shellman's Bluff on the Julienton River. A public boat ramp on Harris Neck NWR (Barbour River Landing) may also be used as a launching site for trips to the island.

Management: U.S. Fish and Wildlife Service, Savannah Coastal Refuges, 912-652-4415

Closest Town: Darien, GA

Additional Information: Contact the refuge office in Savannah to obtain dates for hunts during which the refuge would be closed. Refuge maps, bird checklists, and brochures are available from the Savannah Coastal Refuges office: Dock is for loading and unloading only. Parkway Business Center, Suite 10, 1000 Business Center Drive, Savannah, GA 31405.

64 Rhetts Island

Description: Rhetts Island is a tidewater island with several diked impoundments consisting of about 1,200 acres in the Altamaha River delta. It was one of the original rice plantations that dominated coastal Georgia in the 19th century. Giant cutgrass is the dominant vegetation that buffers the dikes from surrounding Darien and Altamaha rivers. Widgeon grass is commonly found in the ditches that surround the interior of the dikes. Inside the impoundments are grasses and other plants consistent with brackish water marshes that now occupy the old rice fields. Some of the old fields associated with other islands (Butler, Champney, General's) at this site are seasonally drained and planted with grains and then flooded in the fall to provide winter food for the migratory waterfowl that arrive here in late fall by the thousands. Rhetts Island has no vehicle access. Visitors may reach the island by boat. Access points exist around the perimeter of the island where boats may be pulled up and over the dike for access into the impoundment.

Viewing Information: During late fall and winter, Rhetts Island is home to an amazing number of wintering waterfowl. Gadwalls, blue-winged teal, green-winged teal, canvasbacks, redheads, ring-necked ducks, scaups, coots, and many others are found in the impoundment. Bald eagles are frequently seen during all seasons of the year. Osprey are very common and can always be seen. Other wading birds such as great blue herons, wood stork, white ibis, American egrets, great white herons, and clapper rails are all common in the area. Canada geese and snow geese are sometimes seen during the late fall and winter. Rhetts Island is home to a sizeable population of American alligators which may be observed basking in the sun on the dikes. Manatees frequent the Altamaha River area

during the summer and can sometimes be seen feeding on emergent vegetation along the river's edge. Otters may also be observed playing in and around the island. Wildlife viewing is excellent all year at this site. There is an open waterfowl hunting season on a portion of the area, but there are separate viewing areas.

Directions: From Brunswick, travel I-95 to exit 9. Turn east on GA Hwy. 99, then turn north on US Hwy. 17 and travel about 2.5 miles to the Champney River boat ramp. The Rhetts Island impoundment is .5 miles downriver from this boat ramp, on the north side of the river.

Management: Georgia DNR, Wildlife Resources Division, 912-262-3173
Closest Town: Darien, GA

Additional Information: Primitive camp sites are available. A map of the Altamaha Waterfowl Management Area may be obtained from the Georgia DNR at the above phone number. Persons wishing to visit Rhetts Island who are unfamiliar with the area should talk to one of the DNR staff familiar with the area before attempting to visit. At low tide it may be difficult to reach the surrounding dikes from the Altamaha or Darien Rivers as the access points may be without water.

65 Sapelo Island

Description: Sapelo Island, the fourth largest of Georgia's barrier islands, is defined by four dominant habitats: tidal salt marshes (estuaries), upland maritime forests, beach and dune systems and the near-shore waters of the Atlantic Ocean. Dominant flora and fauna characterize each of these habitats and contribute to the total spectrum of wildlife found on Sapelo. The salt marshes are subject to the constant force of 6- to 8-foot tides twice daily. The estuaries of Sapelo, about half the salinity of ocean water, are home to an abundance of resident and migratory species of birds, fish, and

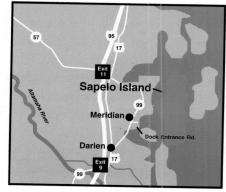

KAREN LAWRENCE

The distinctive habitat types of Sapelo Island are apparent in this bird's eye view of the shoreline.

mammals. The maritime forests are dominated by live oak hammocks, pure stands of slash, loblolly, longleaf and pond pine, and transitional areas that are integrated with pines and oaks. Dense understory species, including palmetto, bay, magnolia, holly, and redcedar create favorable conditions for many forms of native wildlife. Freshwater sloughs are scattered about the island and contain some bottomland hardwoods like maple and sweetgum. Wax myrtle thickets and grasses offer shelter to small mammals and many songbirds.

Viewing Information: Visitors will have opportunities to see wildlife ranging from coastal wading birds to American alligators to white-tailed deer and the occasional wild turkey. The true wildlife gem on Sapelo is the abundance of birds. Neotropical migrants, marsh birds, shorebirds, raptors, game birds, and even off-shore species like the spectacular gannet can be seen while visiting the island. Access to Sapelo Island is limited by the schedule of the island ferry system. Year-round wildlife tours of Sapelo are conducted by the Sapelo Island National Estuarine Research Reserve (SINERR). For the serious wildlife observer, special wildlife viewing tours may be scheduled. In June through September, an additional tour is offered on Fridays to accommodate the peak visitation season.

Directions: From Brunswick, travel I-95 north to exit 9. Turn east on GA Hwy. 99 and travel through Darien 8 miles to Meridian, GA. Follow the signs to the dock entrance road clearly marked on the right.

Management: Georgia DNR, Wildlife Resources Division, 912-485-2251 (SINERR) or 912-437-3224 (Darien Welcome Center)

Closest Town: Darien, GA

Site Notes: tours, observation platforms, interpretive programs, tour fee, ferry fee.

Additional Information: Call the numbers above for detailed information regarding public and group tours.

66 Fort Morris Historic Site

Description: A beautiful coastal retreat where human and natural history abound, Fort Morris Historic Site is a patchwork of varied habitats including spartina marshes, cypress ponds and maritime forests of live oak, southern red oak, cabbage palm, and slash pine. Wonderfully secluded on the Medway River at St. Catherine's Sound, this area offers ample wildlife viewing opportunities.

Viewing Information: Medway River and its banks are teeming with aquatic and coastal wildlife. Wading birds are numerous and seen year-round. Look for snowy egrets, great blue and little green herons, wood storks and anhingas. Bald eagles, red-tailed hawks, and Cooper's hawks can be seen in the fall and winter. Yellow-crowned night herons nest here and can be seen in spring and early summer. The upland forests are excellent for bird watching during spring and fall. Finding a quiet, secluded area for wildlife viewing is easy on this remote historic site.

Directions: From Savannah, travel I-95 south to Midway, GA (exit #13). Turn east and travel 5 miles on Island Highway. Turn left on Fort Morris Road and travel 2 miles to the site.

Management: Georgia DNR, Parks and Historic Sites Division, 912-884-5999

Closest Town: Midway, GA

Site Notes: primitive camping, walking tours, interpretive programs

Additional Information: Site is open Tues. through Sat. from 9 a.m. to 5 p.m. and Sunday from 9:30 a.m. to 5:30 p.m.

67 Gould's Inlet, St. Simons Island

Description: Gould's Inlet is the opening between St. Simons East Beach and the south tip of Sea Island. The inlet is the mouth of Postell Creek. A sandbar extends off the south end of the Sea Island beach out into the inlet, forming its north boundary. This bar, as well as the inlet itself, is a good example of Georgia's barrier island-estuarine interface. The bar changes shape frequently as wind and water energy move the sand. Because of this constant shifting, vegetation cannot grow here permanently, so the bar remains open. The open sand creates a resting place for many species of birds and a feeding site for others.

Viewing Information: This site offers an almost continual coastal bird viewing opportunity. Observation platforms are convenient for wildlife viewing. Migrants and resident species of birds can be seen here. High or incoming tides are best for birding at this site, but something will be there all the time. Binoculars or a spotting scope will give an advantage to the viewer. Resident birds that can be seen every day of the year include brown pelicans, black skimmers, royal terns, laughing gulls, willets, American oystercatchers, and herring gulls. Among the warm-weather visitors, including fall and spring migrants, are black terns, sandwich terns, gull-billed terns, common terns, Caspian terns, reddish egrets, marbled godwits, whimbrels, black-bellied plovers, semi-palmated plovers, Wilson's plovers, western sandpipers, ruddy turnstones, sanderlings, and red knots. Cold-weather birds include cormorants, black-backed gulls, ring-billed gulls, laughing gulls, red-breasted mergansers, Caspian terns, Forster's terns, red-backed dunlins, black-bellied plovers, and piping plovers.

Directions: From Brunswick, travel US Hwy. 17 south. Turn left at and cross the St. Simons Island Causeway. Once on the island, at the large Welcome sign, begin recording mileage. Travel Demere Road through two traffic lights (2.5 miles). Turn left onto East Beach Causeway and continue .5 miles, and turn left on Bruce Drive and travel .7 miles to the end of Bruce Drive and Gould's Inlet.

Management: GA DNR Coastal Resources Division, 912-264-7218

Closest Town: Brunswick, GA

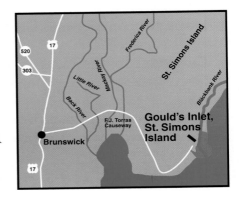

68 Jekyll Island Causeway & Jointer Creek

Description: The causeway to Jekyll cuts through open marsh and mud flats. The area is influenced by tidal waters, with two high tides and two low tides in every day. Spartina grass dominates the saltmarsh vegetation. The Causeway itself has a more diverse plant cover, including wax myrtle, sea ox-eye, marsh elder, and the exotic pink and white oleander, which constitutes an outstanding habitat for marsh rabbits and a variety of other small mammals. At low tide the marsh mud and exposed oyster beds create unique foraging habitats for a wide variety of birds. The Jointer Creek mud flats are seen at low tide exactly 1.8 miles south of the Causeway on US Hwy. 17.

Viewing Information: The Jekyll Island Causeway and Jointer Creek mud flats are good viewing sites for a variety of birds throughout the year. At high tides, the Jekyll Causeway is a good place to see shore and wading birds loafing on the exposed "salt pan" marsh flats situated along the south side of the causeway wherever the grass is sparse. Many different birds can be seen on the wires and telephone poles along the way. Red-tailed hawks, kestrels, osprey, and peregrine falcons can be seen in the fall and winter months. Late October and early November are good times to see flocks of several thousand tree swallows feeding on wax myrtle berries along the causeway. The nearby Jointer Creek mud flats is the most likely site in Georgia to see roseate spoonbills between July and September. It is also a spot to see wood storks, great egrets, and great blue herons during warm weather. This site should be visited during a period of about two hours before or after low tide. Deep silt mud provides good feeding for long-legged birds. Diamondback terrapins can be seen crossing roads between April and July.

Directions: From Brunswick, travel south on US Hwy. 17. Cross the Sidney Lanier Bridge and turn left onto the Jekyll Island Causeway.

Management: Georgia Department of Transportation.

Closest Town: Brunswick, GA

Additional Information: Both the Causeway and US Hwy. 17 present hazards to wildlife viewing because of fast-moving traffic. Caution must be employed, especially when children are present. Binoculars and/or a spotting telescope are highly recommended.

Brown pelicans return to a rookery after fishing.

69 South End Beach, Jekyll Island

Description: This is a typical Georgia beach, with wide, hard-packed sand at low tide and narrow, soft sand at high tide. The beach is characterized by low dunes and a long sloping beach from the high tide line through an intertidal zone to the water's edge. In this intertidal zone from the waterline to the wrack (debris) line will be seen numerous shorebirds and marine animals that wash ashore. This beach is a favorite for wildlife viewing and for beachcombers. Walk south and then west on the beach until you begin to see the transition of the beach to marsh mud and marsh grass. Wildlife activity is at its peak in this transition area.

Viewing Information: An amazing array of wildlife will be visible at this site in the course of a day. Many gulls and terns will add to the "wild" noise of the beach. The makeup of the watchable wildlife also changes signifi-

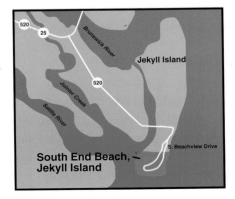

cantly with the seasons. Any time of the year watch for brown pelicans gliding just above the water until they see a meal, causing them to gain altitude dramatically and plummet into the water. You can often see them come up with a catch which they swallow whole on the spot. Binoculars or a spotting scope will help you see more detail in this beach environment. The Atlantic bottle-nosed dolphin is often seen surfacing for air just off shore. Both Wilson's plovers and the American oystercatchers may nest on this beach, but both are very wary so watch from a respectful distance. In winter, migratory waterfowl, including the lesser scaup, bufflehead, ring-necked duck, and migratory birds of prey like the peregrine falcon, the merlin, and the kestrel, are commonly seen near the beach.

Directions: From Brunswick, go south on US Hwy. 17 to the Jekyll Island Causeway (GA Hwy. 50). Enter Jekyll Island through toll booth ($2 fee) and turn right on South Riverview Drive. Follow signs to St. Andrew Picnic Area. Park your vehicle and walk through forest to back beach area. Follow shoreline south to south tip of Jekyll Island.

Management: Georgia DNR, Coastal Resources Division, 912-264-7218

Closest Town: Brunswick, GA

Additional Information: Lodging (hotels) is available on the island.

70 Earth Day Nature Trail

Description: The Earth Day Nature Trail provides an opportunity for a "bird's eye view" of Georgia's outstanding coastal marshes. Georgia's coastal marshlands encompass approximately 378,000 acres in a 4- to 6-mile band behind the barrier islands. These marshes have been identified as one of the most extensive and productive marshland systems in the United States. Developed from lagoons that filled with sediments and deposits from rivers and streams flowing to the ocean, the marshlands of Georgia are a vital part of one of the world's greatest estuaries. Salt marshes are responsible for the continuation and survival of the intricate balance of nature within such estuaries. Producing biomass measuring nearly 20 tons to the acre, a salt marsh like this is four times more productive than the most carefully culti-vated corn. Georgia's salt marshes produce more food energy than any estuarine zone on the eastern seaboard. A variety of marsh grasses flourish in this habitat and are fed from the onrushing tides. The marsh serves as a nursery ground for the growing juveniles of fish and shellfish, and these fish in turn support larger fish.

Viewing Information: Best viewing is early morning or late afternoon, when great numbers of birds are very active and easily seen. Wood storks periodically rest and sun their wings at the edge of a bird viewing pond. You may also see wood storks flying the thermal air currents in the vicinity of the nature trail. The salt marshes are flooded twice daily by the rise and fall of the tide. They are the home or feeding ground of many kinds of marine life, including laughing gulls, great egrets, wood storks, brown pelicans, ospreys, diamondback terrapins, clapper rails, raccoons, willets, red-winged blackbirds, kingfishers, great blue herons, snowy egrets, and marsh rabbits. Plants found along the trail include sea ox-eye, periwinkle, prickly-pear cactus, wax myrtle, redcedar, and smooth cordgrass.

The rare wood stork may be seen soaring high over the marsh.

Directions: Travel south on US Hwy. 17 through the Brunswick City limits. Just north of the Sydney Lanier Bridge, turn left on Conservation Way. There is a sign to the DNR Coastal Regional Headquarters, Brunswick. At northeast end of the parking lot is a sign and entrance to the Earth Day Nature Trail.

Management: Georgia DNR, Coastal Resources Division, 912-264-7218

Closest Town: Brunswick, GA

Site Notes: observation platforms, interpretive programs (self-guided), binoculars available for checkout.

Additional Information: Orientation shelter available for group educational activities. Main building has an aquarium display, wildlife check lists, and blueprints for bird houses.

71 Fort Frederica National Monument

Description: Located on the inland side of St. Simons Island — a coastal barrier island — this colonial town and fort remnants also preserve some beautiful salt marsh and maritime forest habitats. The salt marsh habitat includes discrete zones of "grassland" plants of varying salt tolerance. Bands of cordgrass, salt grass, and needle rush border the Frederica River. Upland of this grassland vegetation is the coastal maritime forest. Here are gnarled live oak and laurel oak draped in Spanish moss, southern magnolia, slash pine, cabbage palm, and saw palmetto.

Viewing Information:

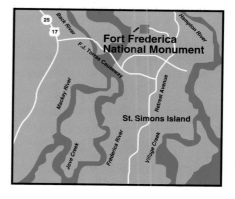

While Fort Frederica is better known for its cultural history, the site offers a great opportunity to appreciate the natural history of one of Georgia's most accessible barrier islands. The borders of the marsh, with concentrations of shrubby understory, provide excellent protected nesting areas for birds and sheltered foraging areas for small animals. River banks and lower salt marshes provide feeding opportunities for shore and wading birds. In addition, the edge of the transition zone between the live oak forest and the partially-cleared town site is utilized by many different species. A variety of birds make Frederica their permanent home, including herons, egrets, and turkey vultures. The occasional kingfisher will skim by, next to the Frederica River, and shrubs are typically full of blue jays, chickadees, and wrens, especially in the winter months. Pileated, downy, and red-bellied woodpeckers abound in the mature forest where insects are easy pickings. White-tailed deer, raccoons, and occasionally an armadillo can be spotted on the forest edge. Early mornings are a good time to catch a glimpse of dolphins cavorting in the river, just off the remains of the old fort's magazine. Pocket gophers, armadillos, broadhead skinks, black racers and flying squirrels might be seen by the lucky visitor. Both scenic and abundant in wildlife, this excellent example of barrier island habitats is worth a visit any time of the year.

Directions: From St. Simons Island causeway, turn left on Sea Island Drive, turn left on Frederica Road and follow the signs.

Management: National Park Service, 912-638-3639 (Monument Office)

Closest Town: St. Simons Island, GA

Site Notes: parking, rest rooms, tours, interpretive programs, entrance fee, tour fee

Additional Information: High temperatures and humidity in the summer months can be challenging; bring a hat, sunscreen, and plenty to drink. Early morning visits can be more pleasant.

72 Cumberland Island National Seashore

Description: Cumberland is an Atlantic coastal barrier island that protects the mainland from the raging ocean storms. This 16-mile-long island contains several typical maritime habitats. The tidal Spartina grass marshes along the inland edge of the island function as nurseries for much of the marine life of the near shore Atlantic Ocean. The interior is live oak or pine canopy with dense palmetto understory opened by trails which are clearly marked and maintained. The dunes are composed of young shifting sands or old forested sands. Interdune meadows separate these two habitat types, the shifting dunes giving way to a spectacularly beautiful beach. Freshwater and brackish water sloughs form between the ancient dunes and provide excellent habitat for American alligators and wading birds.

Viewing Information: One of Georgia's best wildlife viewing areas, Cumberland Island demonstrates tremendous wildlife diversity, especially birds. Tidal marshes are likely to display snowy, cattle and common egrets; wood storks; and great blue, tri-color, green, and little blue herons. Black-crowned night herons and yellow-crowned night herons are rare sights in winter. In winter, large numbers of sparrows, warblers, and hawks will be seen. Peregrine falcons hunting low along the beach are a reasonable winter expectation. Bald eagles are occasionally seen soaring high (possibly with vultures) or sitting in trees or power poles along the marshes. Mammals include white-tailed deer, raccoons, river otters, minks, pocket gophers, and the recently reintroduced bobcat. The most commonly seen marine mammal is the bottle-nosed dolphin, but others may be seen off the beach and in the waterways en route to the island. In mid-summer, prominent beach tracks indicate the previous night's nesting activities of the loggerhead sea turtle. A number of non-poisonous snakes may be seen,

A ghost crab scurries along the beach.

KAREN LAWRENCE

but a more dramatic find would be the diamondback rattlesnake on the roads and in the dunes, or the cottonmouth near the freshwater sloughs. The American alligator is common in freshwater but may also be seen in saltwater. Cumberland has a long history of exotic and domestic animal introductions, as evidenced by the remaining feral horses and feral pigs. Although most of the pigs have been removed, a few may still be seen. Feral horses are more abundant, especially in the dunes and dune meadows where they do considerable damage to the vegetative stability.

Directions: From Brunswick travel I-95 south to exit 2. Travel east on GA Hwy. 40 to St. Mary's. Follow the signs to the waterfront office of the National Park Service. Ferry service to the island leaves from this location.

Management: National Park Service, St. Mary's Office, 912-882-4335

Closest Town: St. Mary's, GA

Site Notes: interpretive programs, observation platforms, rooming house (private)

Additional Information: Call the National Park Service at the number above to make reservations to visit the island. Lodging is available at the Greyfield Inn, a commercial rooming house on the island: 4 North 2nd St., Fernandina Beach, FL 32034. Rain gear and a hat for sun protection are recommended. Sand gnats are ferocious creatures and can ruin a day in the field. Insect repellents are highly recommended. A personal water supply should also be considered essential. The National Park Service owns most of the island. There are private estates remaining, however, and care should be taken to know where you are at all times. Trespassing on private property is strictly prohibited.

73 Okefenokee National Wildlife Refuge

Description: Encompassing an area of approximately 650 square miles, the Okefenokee offers 353,000 acres of designated national wilderness. Habitats on the refuge include open water, wet prairie, shrub-scrub, cypress forest, and upland pine forest on interior islands and perimeter upland areas. The refuge is the headwaters for the St. Mary's River which flows to the Atlantic Ocean, and the famed Suwannee River which drains to the Gulf of Mexico. The name Okefenokee is a native American term that means "land of the trembling earth". Many floating "peat beds" colonize with grasses, shrubs, and trees that move or shake under the weight of a walking person. There are three points of public access to the refuge. Stephen C. Foster State Park, Suwannee Canal Recreation Area, and the privately operated Okefenokee Swamp Park provide good access from all vantage points for casual visitors. Overnight stay or interior travel requires permits and reservations.

Viewing Information: Okefenokee NWR is surely one of the top wildlife viewing areas in Georgia. The potential to observe different species of wildlife is probably greater here than at any other location in the southeastern U.S. A patient and observant watcher can encounter more than 200 species of birds, 50 mammals, and 100 reptiles and amphibians. In the winter, waterfowl abounds, including mallards, ring-necked ducks, wood ducks, black ducks, coots, green-

RICHARD T. BRYANT

Bullfrogs are among the 100 species of reptiles and amphibians that live in the refuge.

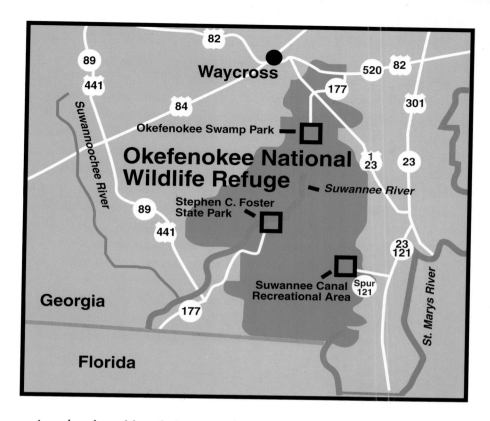

winged teal, and hooded mergansers, which are seen in the prairies along with large numbers of greater sandhill cranes. Ospreys begin nesting. Watch for aerial courtship displays of red-tailed hawks. Brown-headed nuthatches become active at the end of Feb. In spring, purple martins, parula warblers, and eastern kingbirds arrive. Watch for the nesting dances of resident Florida sandhill cranes. Wildflowers begin to bloom as the prairies fill with golden club and bladderworts. Largemouth bass begin to spawn. American alligators are seen sunning on the banks of the water trails. Wading bird rookeries are active. Prothonotary warblers are common along the cypress-lined waterways. Sandhill crane chicks are hatching and ospreys are seen feeding their young in their high bulky nests. American alligators bellow territorial warnings as mating begins.

In summer, the endangered red-cockaded woodpeckers are viewed around their nesting colonies. Florida soft-shell turtles are laying eggs, and raccoons are just as rapidly digging up and eating the eggs. Wild turkey pouts are seen walking in close procession behind their hens. Newborn fawns appear. Young herons, egrets, and ibis, now fully fledged, leave the rookeries. Wood storks are observed feeding

ROBB HELFRICK

in the prairies. Red-headed woodpeckers and pine warblers are seen in pine forest uplands. Nighthawks and chuck-will's widows frequent the evening sky, scooping insects from the air.

In the fall, black bears, white-tailed deer, and turkeys are active, feeding on acorns, nuts and berries. Marsh hawks are seen gliding low over the prairie. Robins and migrating greater sandhill cranes arrive with the cool weather. Watch for the occasional bald eagle perched in the trees or soaring high, perhaps with a group of vultures.

Directions: From Folkston, take GA Hwy 121/23 southwest 8 miles. Entrance will be marked. From Fargo, take GA 177 Spur 16 miles northeast. Follow signs. From Waycross, take US Hwy. 1 south for 10 miles. Entrance will be marked.

Management: U.S. Fish and Wildlife Service, 912-496-7836 (Visitors Center)

Closest Town: Folkston, GA (east entrance)

Fargo, GA (west entrance)

Waycross, GA (north entrance)

Additional Information: For information on facilities, see Stephen C. Foster State Park, Suwannee Canal Recreation Area, and Okefenokee Swamp Park. Overnight wilderness canoe camping (by advance permit only). Freshwater fishing (state regulations apply). Controlled white-tailed deer hunts (advance permit only).

RICHARD T. BRYANT

Water lily

74 Okefenokee Swamp Park

Description: Known as the northern entrance to the Okefenokee National Wildlife Refuge, Okefenokee Swamp Park could also be called the "fast track" or perhaps the "tenderfoot" visit to the great swamp. Excellent wildlife viewing opportunities are found here, although some observations may be made from the comfort of air-conditioned rooms! The principal habitats surrounding the park are cypress, tupelo, and pine flatland. Notwithstanding the added human creature comforts, the world-famous special features of the swamp

The Okefenokee Swamp offers outstanding opportunities for wildlife viewing and quiet reflection.

can be seen here, including tannic "black" waters, large American alligators and other wildlife, as well as the floating peat masses which give the Okefenokee its name, "Land of the Trembling Earth".

Viewing Information: Winter is a great time to watch the wildlife here. There are fewer people on site and many migratory species of wildlife. Fewer American alligators are seen, but a proportionately larger number of otters will be seen fishing and playing along the open water canals. In the spring, wildlife viewing is the best. Wading bird rookeries can be seen from the roads and trails. The continuous feeding causes the young birds to be noisy during all the daylight hours. Good binoculars and telescope are great aids to watching the rookery activity. The available guided boat tour is a good way to see most of the wildlife here. See Okefenokee NWR for more potential wildlife encounters.

RICHARD T. BRYANT

An immature white ibis rests above the blackwaters of the Okefenokee.

Directions: From Waycross, travel US Hwy. 1 south and follow the signs 8 miles to the park entrance.

Management: A private non-profit company leases from the USFWS, 912-283-0583

Closest Town: Waycross

Site Notes: boat tours, boardwalks, observation tower, boat rental, driving trail, fishing

Additional Information: See also the following viewing sites: Stephen C. Foster State Park, Suwannee Canal Recreation Area, and Okefenokee National Wildlife Refuge.

75 Stephen C. Foster State Park

Description: Stephen C. Foster State Park is an 80-acre state facility located in the heart of the Okefenokee National Wildlife Refuge. The park is known as the western access to the 396,000-acre wildlife refuge. The habitats surrounding the park are cypress swamp and pine flatland. Special features of this environment include tannic "black" waters, headwaters of the Suwannee River, and the unstable peat masses floating on top of the water that give the Okefenokee its name, "Land of the Trembling Earth." One can observe the swamp's plant succession from open lake to mature forest, stands of baldcypress and pond cypress trees, and the animal life these areas support, from American alligators to black bears.

Viewing Information: Visitors have access to 25 miles of navigable waterway by renting motor boats or canoes or by launching their own water craft. The interpretive staff conducts three guided boat tours through the swamp every day except Christmas. Viewing the swamp is limited only by inclement weather or extremely low water which would prevent boats from reaching the water, a rare occurrence. Canoe launch and boat ramps are available. See Okefenokee NWR for potential wildlife encounters.

Directions: From Fargo, follow GA Hwy. 94 east across the Suwannee River and turn left on GA Hwy. 177. Travel north 17 miles to park entrance.

Management: Georgia DNR, Parks and Historic Sites Division, 912-637-5274 (park office)

Closest Town: Fargo, GA

Site Notes: tours, interpretive programs

Additional Information: See also: Okefenokee National Wildlife Refuge, Suwannee Canal Recreation Area, Okefenokee Swamp Park.

76 Suwannee Canal Recreation Area

Description: Suwannee Canal Recreation Area is a federal facility located deep in the Okefenokee National Wildlife Refuge. Known as the eastern access to the 396,000-acre wildlife refuge, it is the site of the visitors center. This site provides the best road access to the open water prairies of the Okefenokee. Other habitats surrounding the Area include shrub-scrub forest and cypress domes.

Viewing Information: Visitors will find motorboats and canoes for rent for limited trips along the Suwannee Canal. Slipping along in a ca-

Gray foxes are one of more than 50 mammals found in the Okefenokee Swamp National Wildlife Refuge.

noe provides an advantage to viewing some wildlife forms. Overnight trips also embark from here, but are by permit only and should be arranged in advance. There are both walking trails and driving trails available that offer superb wildlife viewing opportunities. A very special feature is the boardwalk trail, a 1.5-mile round trip over the water to an outstanding observation tower. Dramatic observations such as sandhill cranes are likely on this walk. See Okefenokee NWR for potential wildlife encounters.

Directions: From Folkston, travel south on GA Hwy. 121/23 and follow the signs 8 miles to the entrance.

Management: U.S. Fish and Wildlife Service, 912-496-7156 or 1-800-SWAMP96

Closest Town: Folkston, GA

Site Notes: tours, boardwalks, boat rental, driving trail, fishing

Additional Information: See also: Okefenokee National Wildlife Refuge, Stephen C. Foster State Park, Okefenokee Swamp Park.